The Management of Local Government Records

The Management of Local Government Records

A Guide for Local Officials

Bruce W. Dearstyne

American Association for State and Local History
Nashville, Tennessee

LIBRARY OF CONGRESS
Library of Congress Cataloging-in-Publication Data

Dearstyne, Bruce W. (Bruce William), 1944-
   The management of local government records : a guide for local officials / Bruce W. Dearstyne.
      p.   cm.
   "Where to turn for more help": p.
   Includes bibliographies and index.
   ISBN 0-910050-91-0
   1. Public records—United States—Management. 2. Local government—United States—Records and correspondence—Management. 3. Municipal government—United States—Records and correspondence—Management. I. American Association for State and Local History. II. Title.
JS344.P77D4 1988   88-4004
352.1'64'0973—dc19   CIP

Designed by Gillian Murrey
Cover illustration by Joanne Jaworski

Copyright © 1988 by the American Association for State and Local History. All rights reserved. Printed in the United States of America. Except for brief quotations used in critical articles or reviews, no part of this publication may be reproduced or transmitted in any form by any means, electronic or mechanical, including photocopying, recording, or any information storage/retrieval system, without written permission of the copyright owner. For information, write to The American Association for State and Local History, 172 Second Avenue, North, Suite 102, Nashville, Tennessee 37201.

Research for and publication of this book was made possible by a grant from the National Historical Publications and Records Commission.

Contents

Preface *vii*
Acknowledgments *ix*
1 For the Record *3*
2 Where to Begin *12*
3 Finding Out What's There *23*
4 Records Retention and Disposition *38*
5 Organizing and Controlling Active Records *53*
6 Management of Inactive Records *65*
7 Micrographics and Local Government Records Management *80*
8 Computers and Records Management in Local Government *92*
9 Management of Archival Records *104*
10 Where to Turn for More Help *119*

Appendix. *State Offices With Responsibility for, or Information on, Local Government Records* *133*
Index *143*

Author and publisher make grateful acknowledgement to the sources listed below for permission to use in this book the illustrations specified.

The New York State Archives and Records Administration, New York State Education Department for Figs. 1.1 and 3.2.

Albany County, New York, Hall of Records for Figs. 1.2, 2.1, 4.1 and 5.1.

The State Historical Society, Iowa State Historical Department for Fig. 2.2.

The State Archives, Office of the Secretary of State, Illinois for Fig. 2.2.

The State Historical Society of Wisconsin for Fig. 2.2.

Montgomery County, Ohio, Microfilming and Records Center for Figs. 3.1, 5.2, 6.1 and 7.2.

The Delaware Division of Historical and Cultural Affairs/Bureau of Archives and Records Management for Fig. 4.2.

Bureau of Archives and Records Management, City of Portland, Oregon for Fig. 4.2.

The City of Rochester City Clerk/Records Management Program for Fig. 6.2.

The Tennessee State Library and Archives for Fig. 7.1.

Metropolitan Nashville—Davidson County, Tennessee, Archives, for Fig. 9.1.

Baltimore City Archives and Records Management Office, Maryland for Fig. 9.2.

Preface

*R*ecords are essential by-products of local government activity and, in turn, provide information that keeps government programs going. Local governments could not operate without their records. However, many local officials look at records and see problems: overwhelming volume, too little space, difficult retrieval, inefficiency, and too many tax dollars being spent with little result.

This state of affairs can — and should — be improved. This manual is written for officials who want to solve records problems and manage their records efficiently. It provides guidance and offers practical advice, based on the experiences of local governments that have dealt successfully with managing their records. It covers the basics of records management, introduces advanced concepts, and suggests where to turn for more help. It's not guaranteed to solve all your problems, but it will show where to begin and how to proceed toward sound records programs.

This manual is based on four assumptions:

Local government records are important resources that can and should be managed, just as any other resources of government are managed.

Local officials want to do a good job managing records, but often need information and advice.

Records management techniques are not mysterious or costly and can be applied by any local government.

Records management is a winning proposition for local government — it pays off in cost savings, better information control, and improved preservation of historical records.

This manual is published by the American Association for State and Local History out of a desire to contribute to improved management of local government records, which are among the nation's most important informational and cultural resources. This manual was funded by the National Historical Publications and Records Commission, a federal agency that supports historical records projects, in the hope of promoting improved identification, management, and use of the historically valuable records of local government. The author hopes that this manual will assist local officials in moving from problems to solutions and that, over time, it will lead to better management of records in America's thousands of local governments.

Acknowledgments

Many people contributed to the production of this manual. Indirectly, and over the course of a number years, dozens of local government officials in New York State helped me get ready for it by discussing their records problems and solutions with me in the course of my work in this state. The Joint Committee on the Management, Preservation, and Use of Local Government Records provided oversight and direction in the production of the manual. I am particularly indebted to committee Chair Edward N. Johnson and to several current or former committee members: Richard J. Cox, Gerald Ham, A.K. Johnson, Jr., H.G. Jones, and William S. Price, Jr. At AASLH, Director Jerry George initiated the publication project, James Summerville assisted it on its way, Marilyn Ryall, NICLOG Project Director, was immensely helpful in getting it finished, and Director Larry Tise oversaw its completion. Edward Purcell edited the manuscript.

The managers of two of the most progressive programs in the nation, Robert W. Arnold, III, Executive Director of the Albany County (New York) Hall of Records, and Stephen E. Haller, Records Manager of Montgomery County, Ohio, furnished advice, photographs, and — by example —inspiration for ways to build a strong local records program.

Along the way, many other people assisted by making suggestions, providing materials, or reviewing part or all of the draft, including: Larry J. Hackman, New York State Archives and Records Administration; Margaret Hedstrom, New York State Archives and Records Administration; William G. LeFurgy, Baltimore (Maryland) City Archives and Records

Management Office; David Levine, Ohio Historical Society; John McColgan, Massachusetts Secretary of State's Office; Stanley Parr, City of Portland, Oregon, Records Management Program; Judy R. Reis, City of Tucson (Arizona) Archives; Victor Russell, Records and Archives Division, City of Toronto (Ontario) City Clerk's Office; Sue Holbert, Minnesota Historical Society; and Roy Turnbaugh, Oregon State Archives.

Of course, I am solely responsible for all of the views and advice expressed in the manual.

Finally, I would like to thank my wife, Susan, and my daughters, Annmarie and Emily, for their faith, patience and support during the many months that went into the production of this manual.

Bruce W. Dearstyne

Guilderland, New York
January 1988

The Management of Local Government Records

1
For the Record

When average citizens want to sell property, clear up a tax dispute, get a business license, or settle an estate, they must rely on the efficient management of local government records. Your job — day in and day out — is to take the responsibility for local records, to manage them well and to fulfill an important public trust.

As an official of local government, you are charged with creating order from potential chaos. Records accumulate at an alarming rate, whether in the smallest village or the biggest merged urban-county government, and the challenge of local records management is essentially the same everywhere: to create, organize, maintain, and retrieve important information that allows government and the public to know what happened, to whom, and why.

What exactly do we mean by "local government records?" In most jurisdictions, "records" include practically any type of information received or created during the process of official government business. This means paper documents such as correspondence, memos, ledgers, and deed books, as well as information recorded in newer forms such as sound or video recordings, microfilm, and computer disks or tapes.

Most states have their own legal definition of the term. In Illinois, for example, local government records include: "...any book, paper, map, photograph, or other official documentary material, regardless of physical form or characteristics, made, produced executed or received by any agency or officer pursuant to law in connection with the transaction of public business..."[1]

Local records are protected by law in most states. It's a crime to alter, deface, or mutilate them, and they usually can't be sold or given away without an official act of the government in accord with state legal requirements.

Problems, problems, problems

It's not uncommon to find local government offices suffering from "The Ten Curses of Records Keeping":

- No one is specifically in charge of records. Records are everyone's problem but no one's specific responsibility. Everyone complains about the problem, but no one knows what to do about it.
- Records needed for office business are inadvertently discarded or difficult or impossible to locate when needed. Much valuable time is lost in frustrating and fruitless searches through the files.
- Records needed by outsiders — for instance, state auditors, members of the public with Freedom of Information requests, or attorneys with legal needs — can't be located when requested.
- Office space is crowded with too many records and those no longer needed for day-to-day business are mixed in with those needed every day. The situation gets worse each year — indeed, each business day — as more and more records are created.
- Records no longer needed for any legal or administrative purpose are kept just because no one is sure what should be done with them.
- Older records are banished to attics, basements, closets, and highway garages. No one keeps a listing of them, and after a while, no one knows what records are stored where. Trying to find anything in the accumulated mass of records is a task everyone tries hard to avoid.
- Records are stored in areas where they become covered with dust or dirt, where dry air makes the paper brittle, or where high humidity promotes mold and mildew growth. These conditions speed the destruction of the records and make handling them difficult and unpleasant.
- Records with continuing value for historical and other research are not identified or organized. They become lost among the mass

> of other records and may be destroyed. As a result, important historical developments are obscured or lost sight of entirely.
> • People sense that technological advances such as microfilm or computers can help solve records and information flow problems, but are unsure how to proceed to get the right equipment and systems.
> • Records problems accumulate until a crisis forces action. The records closet gets full, the fire marshal says that something must be done with the old records because they're a fire hazard, a leaky roof soaks the records in the attic, or a broken pipe soaks records in the basement. There is a flurry of action, often wholesale destruction of the accumulated old records. But once the crisis is over, the same records problems continue to build up.

Basic Resources and Public Trusts

Local records are so important it's impossible to imagine life without them. If no one saved official letters, memos, contracts, ledgers, and files, we'd all have to rely on individual memory to handle every transaction or do any work. Government would come to a standstill without records, which are, in effect, its institutional memory. They document the origin, evolution, and operation of government and show how it responds to needs and serves its citizens.

All government officials depend on records from their own files for the information needed for day-to-day management. Effective officials routinely consult records in order to plan, analyze, and track programs. Good records provide officials the right information for decision making.

And, local records document both the rights of citizens and the responsibilities of government. For instance, deed books fix legal ownership and boundaries, wills form the basis for bequeathing and inheriting property, tax records show if land and school taxes have been paid, voting registration and election records prove the right to vote and who won. These and

Fig. 1.1 In many local governments, older records are stored in disorder under poor conditions, accelerating their deterioration and making retrieval nearly impossible. (New York State Archives and Records Administration, New York State Education Department)

many other vital matters are recorded publicly in local government records, available for all to consult.

In addition, many local government records are important sources for research. Lawyers, for example, search local records to substantiate legal points, and public interest groups study the origins of problems and issues. Some records have immense value for historical research and may be the most important sources for the history of the community, its institutions, and the lives of its people.

Records also help to ensure and measure government's accountability. By systematically documenting government operations and performance, records provide a revealing inside look at government and a means for studying its effectiveness and efficiency. This is important in the current era of "open government" and an on-going concern among citizens, journalists, and public administrators.

"Public records are public property, owned by the people in the same sense that the citizens own their courthouse or town hall, sidewalks and streets, funds in the treasury," as one authority puts it. "Indeed, because records document the conduct of the public's business — including the protection of rights, privileges, and property of individual citizens — they constitute a species of public property of a higher value than buildings, equipment, and even money, all of which usually can be replaced..." [2]

What a Records Management Program Can and Should Do:

- Encourage the creation of records that contain accurate, complete, and usable information.
- Ensure that information is recorded and maintained as efficiently as possible.
- Discourage the creation of unnecessary records.
- Minimize the workload on staff who are responsible for filing, maintaining, and retrieving records. Provide information quickly and easily when needed by government officials and the general public.
- Ensure the periodic, systematic, and legal destruction of records that have no further administrative, legal, fiscal, historical or other research value.
- Identify, preserve, and encourage the use of records with enduring value for historical or other research.

Records Management

It's obvious that taking care of local records can't be left to chance. Local governments must manage records, which means seeing to their systematic creation, organization, maintenance, use, and periodic disposition. This is, of course, a tall order, but one that can be filled efficiently and effectively, if you know where to begin and how to proceed.

Fig. 1.2 Local government records constitute the government's "memory" and document its legal rights and responsibilities and those of the people it serves. The primary objective of sound records administration is to make records readily available when needed by government officials and by the general public. (Albany County, NY, Hall of Records)

A full-fledged records management program includes several elements, which fit together and re-enforce each other. It's ideal to develop and apply all these basic elements together, but as a practical matter, you may need to tackle them one at a time. In many cases, putting together a full system of records management may have to be a long-term goal rather than something you can accomplish immediately. Whatever your situation, the elements of a good management program can be developed separately and any of them will be reliable weapons in the battle for better control of records. The basic elements of records management are as follows:

•Sound records management is acknowledged as an important administrative function and is supported by legislators, chief elected officials, and office managers at all levels.

•Overall responsibility for coordinating the records management effort is clearly assigned.

•Employees are trained in the basics of records management.

- Records are retained only so long as needed for administrative, fiscal, legal, historical, or other purposes. They are disposed of periodically in accordance with state legal requirements and guidelines, and within the local government's own procedures.
- Records and information controls, such as correspondence and forms control, filing systems, and indexing and information retrieval systems, are routinely developed and applied.
- Vital records — those essential to the operation and continuity of the government — are given secure protection.
- Inactive records — those no longer needed for office business — are segregated and stored apart from active office space.
- Microfilm is employed where appropriate to improve the dissemination and preservation of information.
- Computers and other modern information technology are used where appropriate to improve the generation, storage, and retrieval of information.
- Archival records — those with enduring value for historical and other research — are carefully identified, preserved, and made available for use.

Records management is not a mysterious science; local governments all over the country have learned how to deal with their records. Taking things step-by-step, it's possible to gain control of local records and to keep control of them so that they are available whenever anyone needs them. The goal, simply put, is "to provide the right information, in the right order, at the right place and time, into the hands of the proper people at the lowest possible cost."[3]

How hard it is to reach this goal will depend on where you begin, but a great deal of help is available in the form of advice and publications. If you study the ideas behind records management and the specific procedures that have proven themselves in the past, then you are well on the road to success.

One of the great benefits of a good records management program — and one often unanticipated — is the overall bargain it provides for local government. Even though it sounds expensive to start up a program, in the long run, records management should save rather than cost money. As one city manager puts it, records management techniques don't depend on "expensive equipment, large personnel costs, or long-term disruption of basic activities. Even at its most basic level, records management will help any organization deal more effectively with information."[4]

Benefits of Records Management

Records management saves money by discouraging the creation of records that really aren't needed in the first place. It cuts down on unnecessary copying and on overhead and expenditures for space.

Records management reduces future costs by ensuring that expensive new equipment, such as microfilm cameras and computers, are not purchased unless these tools will help you manage your information so much better that they repay or justify their costs.

Records management saves space by removing inactive records from busy, crowded offices where space is at a premium, and sending them to storage, and by ensuring the timely destruction of records that are no longer needed.

Records management saves time by ensuring that records are well organized and maintained.

Records management promotes good government by making it easy for program administrators to locate and use information needed to monitor programs, ensure administrative continuity, and make informed policy decisions.

Records management protects the government by ensuring that contracts, agreements, and other records of the government's legal rights and responsibilities are securely protected, well organized, and easily located when needed.

Records management serves the cause of history by identifying and preserving important research records.

Notes

1. Jim Edgar, *Illinois Local Records Management Handbook* (Springfield, 1984), p.1.

2. H.G. Jones, *Local Government Records: An Introduction to Their Management, Preservation, and Use* (Nashville, 1980), pp. 23-24.

3. Edgar, *Illinois Local Records Management Handbook*, "Introduction."

4. William G. LeFurgy, "Records Management: How to Develop a Logical System," *The Office*, (October 1984), 19.

2
Where to Begin

Beyond Problem Solving

Coming to grips with records management typically involves solving problems in stages: first, you take care of the accumulated backlog; then, you tackle the current needs; and, finally, you set the stage to deal with records management in the future.

This manual should help you solve many of your government's past and current records problems. But, a single victory over accumulated paper should be only the beginning. To make sure that the problems do not come back and that records get the care they deserve in the future, local government needs to lay a solid basis for continuing records management. This implies a program built into your government's structure, a program that operates with clear legal authority and has the resources and support needed to do the records management job.

A comprehensive, long-term program is, of course, a worthy goal to shoot for but don't be disheartened if you can't put everything in place instantly. In fact, many local governments have been successful by undertaking records management one step at a time, as money, knowledge, and personnel allow. And, if you decide that you really can't handle everything included in a full records management program, you should feel free to adapt to your own local conditions. It's a good idea in general to strive for a comprehensive program of managing local records, but local governments should decide which elements are most important in their specific circumstances.

Experience shows, however, that successful local government records programs are built on three foundation blocks: legal authority to operate, a specific records management officer in charge, and an advisory committee to provide advice and support.

A Legal Basis for Operation

Your local government records program needs a firm basis of operation — one that's fixed in law. Otherwise, the program lacks clear authority to operate, to secure needed resources, and to enlist the cooperation of everyone in government. A local government ordinance, law, resolution, or some other legal enactment is needed that deals with records management. Your government's legal counsel and the state archival or records management office can advise you on the appropriate form and exact wording, which will depend partly on your state's records laws and on your local government's own charter and legal traditions.

Whatever the form, several elements are important. The ordinance should make clear that records management is a continuing administrative function of the government and it should include a definition of "records" based, if possible, on your state's legal definition. You can also look to the federal government or other local governments for models. The cities of San Diego, Baltimore, and Rochester, for example, have local ordinances that provide good starting points.

The ordinance should list the program's goals and objectives. It should also spell out the program's authority and responsibility — to develop controls for information and records, to segregate and store inactive records, to coordinate disposition, to analyze the potential of automated systems and new technology, and to do whatever other records management tasks you want.

Administrative responsibilities should also be explained. The ordinance ought to either designate a records management officer directly, or provide for such a designation, and detail the person's responsibilities. In addition, it should provide for a records advisory board and indicate its duties. The records ordinance need not be long or complicated. It must, however, be clear and forthright, for it will serve as the basis for records management efforts for years to come.

The Records Management Officer: The Person Who Makes it Happen

As you may have discovered already, records management does not just happen by itself; someone must make it happen. To ensure that the job will get done, one person should be designated as the local government's "records management officer" with clear responsibility to coordinate the records management work.

If yours is a small or medium-sized government, it's unlikely that you will have a trained records manager on staff. Probably you must rely on someone who is willing to learn the rudiments of records management and coordinate records management efforts on a part-time basis. No one can become an expert overnight, but plenty of help is available. By consulting with colleagues, reading about records management, and forming networks for information and advice, it's possible to become very effective. Look at Chapter X, for example, which lists books and organizations to consult.

Larger governments may be able to acquire the services of a full-time, professionally trained records manager. The functional responsibility for records management may be placed with the local government's clerk, chief administrative officer, chief fiscal officer, or elsewhere. Placement is important but even more important is the need for the records management officer to have the support and resources needed to carry out the responsibilities of the position.

The records management officer is not the czar of records;

the job is more like a musical conductor, getting people to work together in harmony. A records management officer doesn't take charge of all of the government's records; instead, he or she works with individual records custodians toward improved records management practices. The officer should not carry out all records-related work directly; rather, he or she should plan, coordinate, and oversee the work.

There is, however, a basic set of responsibilities. The records management officer should:

• Confer with other local government officials in the development and maintenance of a records management program.

• Conduct or coordinate an initial survey and inventory of all records as the basis for planning and launching a program.

• Encourage and coordinate the continuous legal destruction of obsolete records in accordance with state disposition procedures.

• Serve as liaison with the state archival or records office, seeking advice and guidance as needed on records disposition and other records management questions.

• Set up and oversee a program for storage and management of inactive records.

• Review requests for filing cabinets, microfilm equipment, computers, and other records-generating and storage equipment.

• Assist in or coordinate planning for the development of micrographics and computer systems.

• Provide workshops, handbooks, and informal advice as needed for local government employees on records management practices and problems.

• Supervise, or cooperate with, the person in charge of the local government's archival records.

• Report to the chief administrative officer and the local government's legislative body about the records management program's accomplishments and problems.

- Prepare informational statements for the news media and the public on the importance of local government records and the role of the records management program.

Records Advisory Board: Advice and Support

Obviously, a records management officer can't do the job alone. One proven way to assure continuing support is to set up a records advisory board. In fact, some states require the appointment of such local boards to oversee records disposition. Whether required or not, a board can be helpful in many ways. It can guide and promote the overall development of the records management program, act as the program's advocate to enlist cooperation from all departments and agencies, advise the records management officer on the development of the program, review its performance, and make suggestions for changes and improvements. If desired, the board can review proposals for the disposition of records and provide final sign-off before disposition takes place. It can be helpful in advising on the appraisal and identification of records with archival value.

Who should serve on the records advisory board? Members should have an interest in records matters and a measure of influence among their fellow employees. Membership might include the chief executive officer, chief financial officer, clerk, and selected department heads, or their designees. Some local governments include public members on their records boards to provide an outside perspective or to represent the views of users of local government records.

Governmental Leaders: Backing and Resources

No matter how energetic the records management officer, and no matter how supportive the records advisory board, a records management effort won't get far without the active support of the leaders of the government. The local legislative body, chief executive officer, and department heads all need to understand and promote the benefits of records management. Their support is particularly crucial during the start-up phase when the program is still proving itself.

Sometimes it isn't easy to capture the attention of busy lawmakers and administrators, but it is possible. All your powers of persuasion may be called on, especially since education about the importance of records management is usually the first step. You might begin by asking them to read the first chapter of this manual. A good follow-up is to show the audiovisual program "Guardians of the Public Record," available from NICLOG, the publisher of this manual. The program is inexpensive to rent and makes the case for more efficient, less expensive government through records management. The state archival or records management office may be able to help with publications on the advantages of records management programs and speakers who can discuss the issues with local government leaders.

Several of the publications listed in Chapter X can help, and the professional associations noted there also have materials that can help you convince the powers that be that records management is important. One of the best ways of convincing skeptical legislators, mayors, or supervisors, is to have them visit a local government that has set up a successful program, if there is one within travelling distance. Nothing persuades like an example of success that can serve as a model for your own local government.

Of course, once the program is in operation, it can be expected to partially sell itself as it produces cost savings and more efficient information handling. One key factor here will be careful program monitoring and reporting by the records management officer. It's important to report regularly on how the program is going, on the quantity of records disposed of, on savings achieved, on expenditures avoided, on operation of the records center, and on the overall impact of the program.

In any case, to increase a program's success, the leaders of government need to lend support in several ways. First, they should formally establish the program by legal action and designate a records management officer, as discussed above. Second, they should keep the program going with support and resources. Third, they should encourage all government employees to cooperate in meeting records management goals. Fourth, they should set a good example for others by ensuring that their own records receive proper care. And, very important, they should signal their commitment to and recognition of the program through public pronouncements about its operation and results.

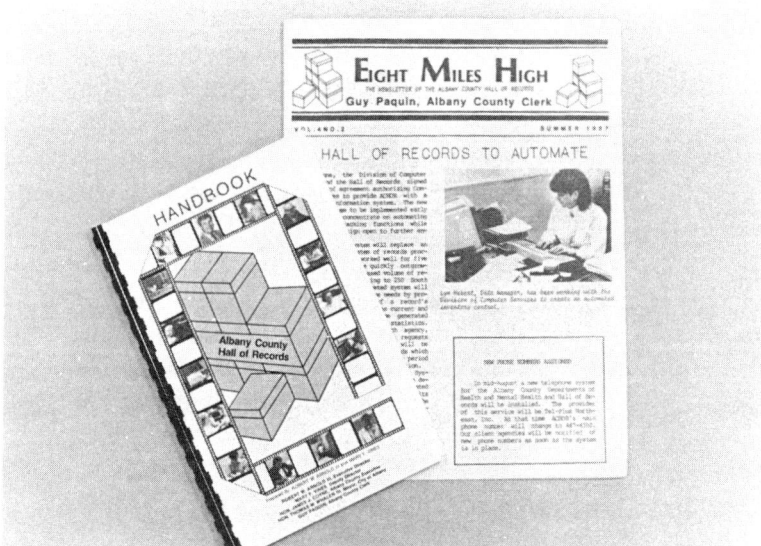

Fig. 2.1 Records management need to be promoted in government in order to garner support from elected officials and to provide service to government offices. A handbook of practices and an informal (but informative!) newsletter can help spread the message throughout the government. (Albany County, NY, Hall of Records)

Winning Public Support

Taxpayer groups, community improvement associations, and other good government groups should be natural allies in establishing better records management. After all, in the final analysis, the records *belong* to the people. Sound records management promotes administrative efficiency, better services, and economy in government — things that citizens, particularly taxpayers, care about! Records provide a means for citizens to scrutinize their government and its programs. The information in public records on individuals, families, property, and businesses, gives citizens a direct stake in their preservation. Finally, given the interest today in family and community history, there should be widespread support for the preservation of local government archival records.

Citizens are a natural reservoir of support for getting local government records management programs started and keeping them going. But getting that support may require an educational effort. Sometimes, it pays to enlist the news media in spreading the gospel of records management. In other cases, it can be done through reports that tout its advantages. The essential messages that citizens need to hear are that records are important and that records management programs will help improve their management.

The State Government's Role

Local government records are essentially local government's responsibility. But state governments have some interest in, and some responsibility for, their sound management. States want to ensure the documentation of state-mandated or supported programs administered through local government, as well as guarantee the availability of records for audit and other oversight functions. They wish to assist efficient local government administrative practices through systematic recordskeeping. States also serve the interests of history and other research by making sure that archival records are

Each state has statutory requirements that affect local government records and their management. It's important to understand these laws when planning and carrying out records management efforts. In some states, legal requirements are consolidated in a local records law; in others, they're scattered in various parts of the legal code.

Somewhere in the state law, you're almost sure to find an official definition of what constitutes a local government "record." There are specific guidelines for disposition of records, probably including a requirement for state approval prior to the destruction of any records. Some states have specific requirements for the protection of records, declare it a crime to deface or steal records, and provide local governments with the authority to seek the return of their records that have been alienated from their custody.

It is common for state laws to provide for microfilming of local government records and for the disposition of some of them after microfilming, with state approval. All of the states have laws that govern public access to records and that prescribe the conditions for release of records with personal or other sensitive information.

Almost every state has an office that is responsible for enforcing the state's local records laws and working with local governments on their records problems. Most of these offices are located in the states' archival or records management programs. For convenience, these offices are listed in Appendix I of this manual. A call or visit to the office in your state may be the best initial step toward improving records management for your local government.

These state offices typically carry out several functions. They regulate the disposition of local government records, either by establishing minimum required retention periods, or through review of requests from local governments that want to throw away records. They may issue records retention and disposition schedules — documents that indicate how long various classes of local government records must be retained.

Fig. 2.2 State archives, records management, or historical offices have important supervisory, oversight, and advisory roles in the area of local government records, including prescribing how long records must be retained. As noted in Chap. 10, several states issue manuals to assist local governments. (Iowa State Historical Department, State Historical Society of Wisconsin, Illinois Secretary of State)

They provide records management advice and assistance through publications, workshops, and consultation visits to local governments. They are a source of technical information in areas such as microfilming and automated data processing.

State offices usually can provide advice on the preservation of records. They can also give advice on how to identify, preserve, and make available local government archival records. Some states, mostly in the Midwest, have a network of officially-designated repositories that will take in and store the archival records of local governments.

A Winning Combination

So, there you have it. Get a records program legally established, appoint a records management officer, and set up an advisory board. Make sure that government leaders are behind the effort and that concerned citizens support it. Operate the program in accord with your state's records laws. Get the best advice and assistance that the experts in the state's archival or records office can give you. With these elements in place, your program stands an excellent chance of high achievement over the long run. The first substantial step forward — finding out what records exist — is discussed in the next chapter.

3
Finding Out What's There

The Next Step

When you have laid the foundation of a records management program with an ordinance, a program officer, and perhaps an advisory board, it's time for the first specific step: taking an inventory to find out just what records exist. The results of the inventory will allow you to decide which records to keep and which to discard. If your state issues records retention and disposition schedules for local governments, you can compare the inventory results to the schedule. If your state does not issue schedules, you can use the results of the inventory to create a schedule for your local government alone; the box at the end of this chapter explains how.

Taking an inventory and making sure that your organization has a good records retention schedule will help you to plan other records management activities. For example, you'll be able to organize the records and establish filing systems and other controls so that everyone who needs information can find it and so that the records situation does not get out of control again.

It makes sense to take an inventory, for how can you take control of records without knowing how many there are, how active and how old, how quickly they accumulate, and how important they are to the office that produced them and to the public? It may take a major effort, but the results should be worth it — provided that the inventory is used as the basis for planning and *action* to alleviate records problems and develop sound records management efforts.

The Informal Survey

Before attempting a full-blown inventory, it's probably a good idea to do an informal survey of records, as a way to get an overview of records and storage problems. A survey also gives an opportunity to talk things over with department heads, office managers, clerks, and secretaries. The survey should aim for general answers to several questions. Where are most of the records located in the offices? How many records are there, and how fast are they accumulating? What major filing systems are people using? What records are located outside of offices — in basements, attics, and other storage areas? What are their volume and condition? How is records disposition handled?

The survey can also turn up additional information: who

Fig. 3.1 Inventorying records requires planning, cooperation, accuracy, and a determination to include all the records. The inventory's results are then used for important decisions on retention and disposition of records and as the basis for additional planning. (Montgomery County, Ohio, Microfilming and Records Center)

is in charge of records in the various offices? What records management practices are already in place? What are the most pressing problems?

Asking about these things informally will give you a birds-eye view of what to expect during the full inventory. It will make planning much easier and will guide you in taking on the next steps. And, in the course of the survey you have a great chance to make yourself and your project known to co-workers in government.

Gathering the Evidence: The Inventory

The informal survey prepares everyone for what's coming next: the formal records inventory. The inventory aims to identify the types, quantities, and locations of all records and to gather additional information on records storage equipment, on who creates the records, why they're created, who uses them, how long they're likely to be needed, and how their management might be improved.

The inventory must gather enough information for later analysis and planning, but must not bog down in too much detail. For instance, an inventory form that describes something as broad as "Miscellaneous Correspondence" or "Fiscal Records" is not of much use. On the other hand, there will not be enough time (or patience), and there is no real need, to list every individual folder and volume. The best middle ground is to inventory by records *series*. Series are file units that are created, arranged, and maintained as a unit because they relate to a particular subject or function, result from the same activity, have the same form, or are related to each other in some other apparent way. In other words, they are records that belong together. They can and should be inventoried as units and can be transferred and disposed of as units.

Series are the most common categories of records in most offices, and they are usually the basis for office filing systems.

They are naturally related to the history, organization, and functioning of the offices that produced them. In a city purchasing office, for instance, you might expect to find these major series: Purchase Requisitions; Purchase Orders; Receiving Reports; Bids, Successful; and Bids, Unsuccessful. A county tax collection office would have series that include Tax Rolls, Receipt Books, and Statements of Unpaid Taxes. A town building office's files probably would include series such as Applications and Permits; Certificates of Occupancy; Permit Ledgers; and Permit Fee Receipts. A village personnel office might have Civil Service Exam Announcements; Personnel Folders; and Worker's Compensation Folders. It takes some records experience to be able to identify series easily and consistently. But office personnel — the people who know the records best — can help.

A records inventory is more than just a stock-taking and listing. It's a major effort to identify, describe, and record basic information about every series of records that the government produces. After the inventory is completed, in conjunction with office heads, the records manager will be able to determine the nature and value of each records series and then proceed to create a records retention schedule (if one hasn't been provided by the state archives).

The Inventory Form

A clear, concise, carefully designed inventory form is a necessary tool for gathering and analyzing the information. When filled out, the form gives information to study and analyze. The form needs to be easy to use, no more than a single page, but with enough space for basic information on the series title, dates, volume, description of content and use, location, and suggestions about how long the records should be maintained and why. It should also have a space for noting what action was taken as a result of the inventory.

A sample form along with suggestions about how to use it are included at the end of this chapter. If you like the form, just duplicate and use it. But there is nothing that says you can't go ahead and design your own form that better fits your own situation. The important thing is to make sure that the form has space for all the information that is needed and that it is used in the same way for the entire inventory.

Doing the Work

A good form and a clear goal are important, but other ingredients are also needed to make the inventory a success. An inventory requires the assistance and cooperation of many people. The work can be frustrated or defeated because people are possessive about "their" files, because they don't understand why the inventory is being done, and the records retention schedule created, or because they feel they don't have time to help. Overcoming these obstacles usually calls for a combination of authority and persuasion. The relationships you established during the informal survey can help a lot. It's a good idea, at the outset, to make sure that the inventory has the backing of the top officials. The mayor, supervisor, or other chief executive officer, can smooth the way with a message to all employees that outlines the inventory's goals, tells how it will be carried out, and asks for everyone's support and cooperation.

Someone has to be in charge of the inventory and it's a logical assignment for the records management officer. Having the records officer in charge also helps ensure that the work will get done, and on time. In a small unit of government, the records officer may actually fill out the forms. In larger governments, it probably makes sense to designate one person in each department or office to do it. The records officer can train these people in how to identify series and fill out the forms. He or she can also coordinate the work, review the completed forms for accuracy and completeness, and keep the entire effort moving smoothly.

It's useful to establish, and keep to, a timetable, and strive to make the inventory complete. *All* the records should be covered by the inventory, including those that people may think of as just "housekeeping" records stuffed away on shelves. Don't skip over or leave out any records just because of pressure to get the inventory finished.

Begin the inventory work with the most recent records, the active office files, and then go on to older records in storage areas. Office personnel usually find it easier to answer questions about the purpose, value, and uses of their current records. Getting down the information on these records first will make it easier to identify and record information on the older files stored out-of-office.

Using the Results

An inventory should lead to much more than only a one-time "housecleaning." Instead, the completed forms can be viewed as *action* documents. The records management officer, working with agency heads and office managers, should carefully study the forms and use them for making decisions on how to improve records management for the long run. This needs to be done as soon as possible after the inventory is completed, before interest wanes, and before substantially more records accumulate that will need additional work.

Probably the most immediate use for the inventory is as a basis for deciding on retention and disposition of records following state schedules, or preparing your own schedule. Specific steps that tell you how to do this are included at the end of this chapter, and records schedules are discussed in more detail in Chapter IV. In effect, the inventory and the records retention schedule will guide you in what to keep and what to discard. This will allow you to identify and dispose of obsolete records that have met approved minimum required retention periods, in accordance with state and local legal requirements. And if your local government is like most, the inventory will turn up many records that can be discarded and, as a result, lead to the disposal of many pounds (tons?)

of unneeded records and the freeing of many filing cabinets and considerable storage space.

Records disposition is an important result of the inventory, but the completed forms also have many other uses in building a records management program. This is especially true when the inventory form has been designed so that it includes information that allows you to do the following at the conclusion of the inventory project:

- Review production, use, and storage of duplicate copies of records, e.g., multiple copies of forms or carbon copies of correspondence or reports. Make recommendations for discontinuing unnecessary copies.
- Identify records that duplicate or provide essentially the same information as other series. Consider consolidating these series or discontinuing one or more of them.
- Locate filing cabinets and other records storage equipment that are being underutilized or that can be emptied and reused.
- Identify records that are not consulted frequently and that could be moved to an inactive storage facility.
- Determine which records need better filing, indexing, or other access and control systems to make them more readily accessible and usable.
- Decide which records are most appropriate for microfilming.
- Identify archival records and make plans for their preservation and management.
- Note records storage areas that are unsuitable for continued use due to lack of security, poor temperature and humidity controls, or other reasons.
- Identify secure storage areas that are suitable for long-term storage of inactive records or for archival records.

The records management officer should note on the inventory itself which, if any, of the above listed actions were taken. (The sample form provided in this chapter has a specific section just for this purpose.) The completed forms should then be filed to show what records existed at the time of the inventory and what actions were taken.

To implement inventory follow-up measures, you may want to develop a formal action plan. This plan should identify specific goals and objectives to be achieved resources that will be needed, and a timetable for the work.

A Successful Finish

There is one final step that should not be neglected. A report should be made to the local government's chief executive officer and legislative body on the findings and conclusions of the inventory and on what major steps were taken as a result of it. The report is a good way to wrap up the inventory effort. It draws attention not only to the inventory and the records retention schedule, but also to the results of the project and the implication for the future.

It is particularly important to document the savings, both in time and money, that the inventory produced. Nothing garners support like a demonstration of savings and heightened efficiency.

The records inventory project is a giant step forward for any records management program. With the results of the inventory in hand, you're ready to continue the momentum and build the program. The next chapter discusses concepts that are important in implementing an inventory and retention schedule project and in developing and managing a records management program as well.

INSTRUCTIONS FOR RECORDS INVENTORY AND ANALYSIS FORM

Introduction

This form is adapted from New York State Archives, *Managing Local Government Records* (Albany, 1985). It may be copied and used by any local government official, or it may be modified to include more or less information.

It is advisable to fill out one form for each series of records that is found in each location. After the inventory is completed, the forms can be used to match parts of the same series that exist in different locations. The completed forms should be retained permanently because they document what records existed at the time of the survey, and the steps needed or taken to improve the management of the records.

FILLING OUT THE FORMS AND USING THE RESULTS

The following is a commentary on each of the 20 elements that are found on the form.

1. *Department/Division/Section.* This information indicates the department and/or the program that created the records. This is important in determining the origin, nature, and purpose of the record. It also indicates who has custodial responsibility for the record.

2. *Title of Records Series.* This identifying information should be as precise and descriptive as possible. Often, it is helpful to: (a) indicate the title that appears on forms if the series is made up of forms; or (b) indicate the title that appears on volumes or on file folders; or (c) put down a title from the appropriate records retention and disposition schedule, if there is one that covers the records. In writing a new records series title, remember that it will usually consist of a record type and an identifying attribute. (i.e. - correspondence = record type; mayor = identifying attribute; record series title = correspondence of the mayor).

   Location). Indicate the physical location; e.g. room and file cabinet, shelf, etc., of the records. This information, together with that in items 15 and 17, will provide a basis for analyzing the adequacy of existing storage areas and the need for new or improved storage space or procedures.

4. *Description of records series.* This is perhaps the most important information recorded on the form. It should include informa-

RECORDS INVENTORY AND ANALYSIS WORKSHEET

1) Department	Division	Section

2) Title of Records Series

3) Location of Records

4) Description of Records Series (content, purpose, etc.)

5) Earliest Date/Latest Date	6) Records still created? YES ☐ NO ☐	7) Volume _____ cu. ft.	8) Annual Accumulation _____ cu. ft.

9) Record Series Characteristics (Check Appropriate Boxes)
TYPE: ☐ PAPER   ☐ CARD   ☐ BOUND VOLUME   ☐ MICROFILM   ☐ MACHINE READABLE
      ☐ OTHER (Specify) _____
SIZE: ☐ LETTER   ☐ LEGAL   ☐ OTHER (Specify) _____
STATUS: ☐ ORIGINAL   ☐ COPY
FORMAT: ☐ TYPEWRITTEN   ☐ HANDWRITTEN   ☐ OTHER _____
ARRANGE-
MENT: ☐ CHRONOLOGICAL   ☐ ALPHABETICAL BY _____   ☐ NUMERICAL BY _____   ☐ OTHER _____

10) Reference Frequency (check blocks, insert numbers, circle appropriate words)
_____ Times, daily, weekly, monthly, yearly for _____ months, years   Never after _____

11) Information Available Elsewhere? YES ☐ NO ☐ (If yes, where? _____)	12) Microfilmed? YES ☐ NO ☐ (If yes, explain _____)

Fig. 3.2. This Records Inventory and Analysis Worksheet, the instructions on pages 31, and 34-36, can be used to take your own records inventory. If you like this form, simply duplicate it or adapt it to your own needs.

13) Are records indexed?

　　YES ☐　NO ☐　(If yes, identify _____)

14) How stored?

　　☐ Filing Cabinets　☐ Shelves　☐ Boxes　☐ Other _____

15) Condition of Records

　　____ Poor　____ Fair　____ Good　(Explain any problems) _____

16) Records on State Archives' Records Retention and Disposition Schedule?

　　YES ☐　NO ☐　If yes, Schedule No. _____ Item No. on Schedule _____

　　If no, suggested retention period and justification _____

17) Condition of Storage Area (security, fireproof, alarms, environment, etc.)

　　☐ Good　☐ Poor　State any storage problems _____

18) Additional Comments _____

19) Name of Person Completing Inventory _____ Date _____

20) Action taken

　　☐ Records disposed of, date _____.　☐ Microfilmed, date _____.

　　☐ Sent to inactive records center, date _____.　☐ Retain permanently, sent to archives, date _____.

　　☐ Other (Explain) _____

21) Name of person taking action _____

From: *Managing Local Government Records: A Manual for Local Government Officials in New York State* (Albany: State Education Department), 1985.)

tion on: (a) Purpose - why was the record created? What program activity or transaction was it intended to document? (b) Content— what information is found in the record? and (c) Use — how has the record been used and for what purpose?

5. *Earliest/latest date.* This is important when making decisions on retention and disposition and in checking other locations for earlier or later parts of the same series.

6. *Records still created?* This is useful information for determining the importance of the records, for projecting future growth and storage needs, and in making decisions about the need for controls such as filing and indexing systems.

7. *Volume.* This is the quantity of the records in terms of cubic feet. The accompanying list of "CUBIC FOOT EQUIVALENTS" will be of assistance in determining the volume. The measurement of volume is important in judging the significance of the records as storage problems and in documenting volume of records disposed of.

8. *Annual accumulation.* This is the volume (in cubic feet) of records created annually, for records that are still being created. It is an important measurement of current records storage needs and is also crucial in estimating future records storage needs including an inactive records storage area or microfilming of the records.

9. *Records series characteristics.* The type, size, status, format, and arrangement of records are important characteristics for understanding their nature and determining storage needs.

10. *Reference frequency.* How often are the records used? Frequent use may indicate a need for evaluation of the adequacy of indexing, filing, and other information access systems. Infrequent use may suggest the need to move the records from active office areas to inactive records storage areas or to legally dispose of them.

11. *Information available elsewhere?* Is the information duplicated in another series? Is it summarized or presented in more detail in another series? The answers will affect decisions on the retention and disposition of the records.

12. *Microfilmed?* Have the records been microfilmed? If so, is there a sound reason for filming them? Does the microfilm meet acceptable standards?

13. *Indexed?* Records that are frequently referenced and that lend

themselves to indexing might be considered for installation of an indexing system.

14. *How are the records stored?* It is important to identify the type and amount of equipment used. This provides a basis for estimating storage costs. It also permits an estimate of how many filing cabinets or how much shelf space will become available for reuse if records are moved or disposed of.

15. *Condition.* A descriptive explanation of physical condition of the records will later serve as a basis for decisions on the adequacy of the storage environment and for conservation measures that may need to be taken to stabilize, preserve, or restore selected archival records. It is particularly important to note problems such as brittleness, water damage, mold, mildew, insect or rodent damage, etc.

16. *Records on Retention and Disposition Schedule?* Are the records covered by an existing, approved records retention and disposition schedule? If not, a suggested retention period should be indicated along with an indication of *why* that period seems appropriate. The justification should make reference to the administrative, fiscal, legal, and historical or other research value of the records.

17. *Condition of storage area.* This information is important in judging the adequacy of the storage area. It should be used in conjunction with the information in items 3 and 15.

18. *Additional comments.* Make any additional comments that will be helpful in describing the records, in indicating records management considerations, or in helping make decisions on how to improve their management.

19. *Person completing the inventory.* Record the name of the person completing the inventory and the date of the inventory.

20. *Action taken.* This item is important for long-term documentation of records management decisions. It is important to record here what action was taken in regard to the records as a result of the analysis of the information gathered on the form. Were the records disposed of? Microfilmed? Sent to an inactive records center? Transferred to the local government archives? Was their creation discontinued? Was their format or content changed? Was access improved through installation of an indexing or filing system? Indicate here these or any other actions taken.

CUBIC FOOT EQUIVALENTS
(For use in filling out inventory form)

File Folder Drawers	Cu. Ft.
Letter	1.5
Letter Transfile	2.0
Legal	2.0
Legal Transfile	2.5
Ledger	3.0
Jumbo	4.0

Shelf Units	
Letter 36" long	2.4
Legal 36" long	3.0

Card File Drawers	
3" x 5" x 26" long	0.4
3" x 5" x 14" long	0.2
3 ½" x 7 ½" x 26" long (tab)	0.4
3 ½" x 7 ½" x 14" long (tab)	0.2
4" x 6" x 26" long	0.5
4" x 6" x 14" long	0.2
5" x 8" x 26" long	0.7
5" x 8" x 14" long	0.4
6" x 9" x 26" long	1.0
6" x 9" x 14" long	0.6
8" x 8" x 26" long	1.2
8" x 8" x 14" long	0.6

Map or Plan Drawer	Cu. Ft.
2" x 26" x 38" (flat)	1.1
2" x 38" x 50" (flat)	2.2
4" x 26" x 38" (flat)	2.3
4" x 38" x 50" (flat)	4.4

Map or Plan Tubes	
2" x 2" x 38" (roll)	0.1
2" x 2" x 50" (roll)	0.1
4" x 4" x 38" (roll)	0.3
4" x 4" x 50" (roll)	0.5

Record Center Containers	
10" x 12" x 15" (standard 1 cu. ft. records center carton)	
3 1/2" x 8" x 14" (tab)	
3 1/2" x 8" x 24" (check)	
6" x 6" x 36" (map)	
6" x 6" x 48" (map)	
4" x 4" x 48" (map)	

All Other — Use Formula
L x W x H (inches) = *cu. ft./unit 1728"*

How to Get From an Inventory to a Records Retention Schedule

If your state archives or records management office has not issued a records retention and disposition schedule for your local government, you may wish to use the inventory to create your own. It's essential that you ensure the schedule complies with local and state legal requirements and that its use is approved locally and by the state before it is used to dispose of records. Here are the steps to follow:

1. Gather together all completed inventory forms.

2. Sort inventory forms into groups that have the same record series title.

3. Rewrite and combine titles if necessary.

4. On a records analysis form (or the inventory form itself) for each record series, indicate a recommended retention period. Recommended retention periods should be based on an application of appraisal values as discussed in Chapter IV and should take into account administrative, fiscal, legal, and research use of the records. In addition, you may want to check with other local governments to see how long they keep similar types of records.

5. Send the completed records analysis forms for review to the department whose records were inventoried. If the department personnel want to revise the proposed retention period for a series, ask them what their justification is for doing so.

6. Once the department has responded, make final adjustments to the records analysis forms, and then write the records retention schedule. This should consist of a listing of each series title and the retention period.

7. Send the completed draft records retention schedule to the department for review.

8. After the department review, make any adjustments that are necessary.

9. Determine the process within your local government for getting the records retention schedule approved. This may require obtaining approval from one or more of the following: the local government's clerk, chief executive officer, council or governing body.

10. Secure approval from the state archives or records management program or other state authority as required by your state's records laws.

4
Records Retention and Disposition

Retention and Disposition:
A Central Records Management Concern

Modern day local government "is by its service nature a paperwork factory. Requirements for the creation, reception, maintenance, and retrieval of information comprise a large, continuous responsibility and burden ..."[1] Indeed, in some cases, the rapid accumulation and sheer volume of records literally threaten to drive local government employees out of their offices. That is why the objectives of a records program should be "to make the records serve the purposes for which they were created as cheaply and effectively as possible, and to *make a proper disposition of them after they have served those purposes*"[2] (emphasis added). The systematic disposition of records, discussed in this chapter, needs to be a core element of any successful records management program.

In planning for records disposition, it is useful to think of records as passing through a "life cycle." The first stage is *creation* — information is received or generated and recorded for the first time, bringing the record into existence. The record then enters an *"active"* phase. It is filed for easy retrieval and is used frequently. In time, however, the record has served the primary purpose for which it was created, and it is no longer needed frequently and passes into an *"inactive"* phase. Inactive records are not yet candidates for disposition, but they can be segregated from active records for management efficiency, as discussed in Chapter VI.

Finally, the records enter their last phase — *disposition.* Most

Fig. 4.1 Local governments in the United States create or receive millions of new records every year in the normal course of carrying out governmental business and serving the public. Decisions on retention and disposition are a central concern of records management programs. (Albany County, NY, Hall of Records)

records become obsolete; that is, they cease to have usefulness for public business and possess no enduring value for historical or other research. What began as a useful information tool becomes a spent informational resource and a useless storage burden. For these records, "disposition" should mean outright destruction, in accordance with legal requirements. A small amount, usually 5 percent or less, possess enduring value because of the information they contain for administrative, legal, or historical or other research. For these records, commonly called "archival records" or simply "archives," "disposition" should actually mean transfer to the local government's archival program, discussed in Chapter IX.

Systematic Retention and Disposition: Advantages

A systematic approach to records retention and disposition along the lines discussed in this chapter, will bring several benefits:

- Ensure that records are retained and available as long as needed for administrative, fiscal, legal, and historical and other research purposes.
- Provide for the prompt and continuing disposal of records no longer needed for these purposes, relieving local government of the burden of storing them.
- Free records storage space and equipment to accommodate new records as they are created.
- Reduce time and effort required to sort through unneeded records in search of items needed for current business.
- Eliminate storage problems and possible fire hazards associated with large quantities of old records.
- May make it unnecessary to resort to microfilming as a space-saving measure.

When records are retained past the point they might be needed for any conceivable public business or research use, storage problems mount, storage costs increase, and information retrieval is thwarted. Yet that is exactly what happens in many local governments. Officials are reluctant to discard any records on the assumption that someone, someday might need them, the decision on what to do with records is postponed until some future time. Or, officials may not fully understand legal retention requirements, and rather than attempting to go through the prescribed disposition process, they elect to retain everything. Actually, when records retention periods are based on realistic, informed assessments, future problems are unlikely to occur.

Retention and Disposition: the State's Role

Every state has legal requirements covering retention and disposition of local government records. As noted in Chapter III, these requirements spring from the states' responsibilities to ensure that records are retained for local government administration, for state oversight responsibilities such as audit, and for long-term historical and other research. Requirements and disposition procedures vary from state to state. Even within a state, there may be individual laws that establish specific retention periods for certain categories of records. The state archives or records management office may handle most disposition questions but other offices may have jurisdiction in some cases, —the state office of court administration, for example, may oversee court records. It is advisable to check with the state agency in Appendix I for up-to-date information.

Many states publish records retention and disposition *schedules* for local government records. A schedule is "a document governing, on a continuing basis, the retention and disposition of the recurring records series of an agency or organization."[3] There may be one schedule for all town records, one for cities, one for counties, one for schools, and so on. The schedules are prepared by state records analysts after examination of local government records and consultation with local officials. Schedules list records, specify how long they must be kept and, in some cases, indicate conditions (e.g., "after supersession," "after expiration," or "after state audit") that must be satisfied before records are destroyed. In most cases, schedules must be adopted by local governments through a formal resolution or other official action, and the consent of the issuing state agency must be secured to their use, before they may be used for disposition of records. The schedule remains in effect, however, until rescinded or superseded by the issuing state office.

In other states, local governments must initiate their own records retention and disposition requests. This approach gives local officials more initiative, but it requires them to carefully review and analyze their records to arrive at realistic proposed retention periods. State permission must be secured before disposition is carried out, usually through one of two routes. The first is for local governments to develop

STATE OF DELAWARE
DIVISION OF HISTORICAL
AND CULTURAL AFFAIRS
BUREAU OF ARCHIVES
AND RECORDS MANAGEMENT
HALL OF RECORDS
DOVER, DELAWARE 19901

COUNTY
GENERAL RECORDS RETENTION SCHEDULE
FINANCIAL SECTION

Page 6 of 26

APPROVED: _[signature]_
STATE ARCHIVIST AND RECORDS ADMINISTRATOR
EFFECTIVE DATE: August 1, 1987

Item No.	Record Title and Description	Vital	Recommended Retention Period
11.00	**Check Vouchers File** Usually extra "accounting copies" of checks drawn on county accounts, often with vouchers attached. Voucher portion is used to describe or designate the purpose for which the check is drawn. Generally shows invoice date, invoice number, voucher number, amount, discount and net, to whom issued, check number, and amount of check. These records serve as a cross-reference to the Accounts Payable Files.		3 years.
12.00	**DAILY CASH RECORDS**		
12.01	**Daily Cash Accounting Records** Adding machine tapes, register or cash drawer reconciliations, transmittal reports, and similar records used to compile or support daily cash reports.		3 years.
12.02	**Daily Cash Reports File** Generally contains a record of cash balances, receipts and disbursements completed during the day.	Yes	5 years.
13.00	**Designation of Bank or Other Depository for County Funds** Description of condition of county funds deposited in bank.		7 years after termination.
14.00	**Statement of Bond or Other Collateral Security Posted by Bank or Other Depository of County Funds**		1 year after final audit.
15.00	**Bank Deposit (Pass) Book Checking/Savings** Amount, description of transaction, date and current balance of account in bank.	Yes	7 years after date of last entry.

Fig. 4.2 Legal retention and disposition requirements for local government records vary from state to state. Some states issue comprehensive records schedules for their local governments, as illustrated by the page from the Delaware schedule for counties. In other states, localities seek disposition approval from the state or develop their own schedules, secure state approval, and apply them

DECEMBER 1980

CITY OF PORTLAND
RECORDS CONTROL SCHEDULE

SCHEDULE NUMBER	DESCRIPTION OF RECORDS	RETENTION AND DISPOSITION
4806-04	ACCOUNTS RECEIVABLE STATUS REPORTS. Includes validation, issues, payments, aging, outstanding and update control reports. AUDIT WORTHY.	3 years. Retain in office through audit then transfer to City Records Center.
4807	ACCOUNTS PAYABLE.	
4807-01	OPEN VENDOR FILE. Claim file consisting of encumbering and accounting copies of purchase orders to which are added bills, invoices, statements, payment authorizations and reports of receipts of goods or services. The processing of these records produces warrants. Open vendor file is arranged alphabetically by vendor name. AUDIT WORTHY.	Hold through processing.
4807-02	GENERAL WARRANTS. Accounts Payable (pink) copy of warrants issued. Filed in warrant number sequence.	2 years.
4807-03	SIGNATURE VERIFICATION FILE. Record of signatures authorized to sign input documents to Accounts Payable system. The signatures are accumulated at the beginning of each fiscal year. AUDIT WORTHY.	7 years after superseded.
4807-04	CONTRACTS PAYABLE LEDGER. Manual subsidiary ledger for recording payments on contracts. Arranged alphabetically by name of contractor. AUDIT WORTHY.	6 years after payment or cancellation of obligation.
4807-05	CONTRACTS PAYABLE WORKING FILE. Includes contracts payable backing sheets for general fund and CETA fund.	1 year following payment or cancellation of obligation.

in accord with state law. The page from the retention schedule developed by the City of Portland, Oregon, as part of its comprehensive records management and archival program, illustrates this approach. (Delaware Division of Historical and Cultural Affairs/Bureau of Archives and Records Management, and City of Portland, Oregon) their own schedules and submit them to state records authorities for review and approval. Once that approval is given, the schedule continues in effect until approval is withdrawn by the state or the schedule is superseded by the local government itself. The second route is for local governments to request permission to destroy specified records. This permission is sometimes called a "one-time disposal authorization" since it covers only the records specified in the local government's request.

In some states, the pattern is mixed. There are state-issued schedules for the most common records but local governments must develop and secure state approval of their own schedules, or secure "one time" authorizations, for records not covered by the state schedules.

Appraising Records: an Analytical Process

How long should records be retained? The answer is derived by carefully *appraising* records. Appraisal is "the process of determining the value and thus the disposition of records based upon their current administrative, legal, and fiscal use; their evidential and information or research value; their arrangement; and their relationship to other records."[4] The appraisal process is essentially the same whether carried out by a records analyst from the state archives office or by a local government's records management officer. It requires an understanding of the organization and functioning of government programs and of the documentation they produce. It necessitates examination of records to distinguish those that reflect policy making and important activities from those that cover routine administrative activities and thus have only passing significance. Appraisal requires at least four lines of analysis:

• *Function and purpose.* Why was the record created? What purposes does it serve? What governmental functions are dependent on its existence?

• *Informational content.* What information does the record

contain? How significant is the information for present and probable future uses?

• *Use.* Who uses the records now, and for what purposes? Who is likely to use it in the future?

• *Uniqueness.* Does the information in the record exist elsewhere? If so, is it in a form that is easily usable?

Appraisal is usually carried out at the series level and results in a retention period being established for each series. Much of the information needed for appraisal of existing series should be available from the initial records inventory, described in Chapter III. The appraisal process should concentrate on determining the importance or "values" of records as a basis for establishing retention periods for them. It is helpful to determine the degree of two different types of values, often called "primary" and "secondary" values, discussed below.

Appraising Records: Primary Values

The "primary" value of records is their importance to the agency that created or assembled them, for continuing administrative, operational, and other purposes. In general, there are three kinds of primary values: administrative, fiscal, and legal.

Administrative value

A record possesses administrative value "if it helps the office perform its current work or would help the office in the performance of future work."[5] Records have administrative value so long as they are needed for conduct of the business to which they pertain or if they establish policy or document operations and are therefore essential for administrative consistency and continuity. Examples of records with considerable administrative value are directives, orders, regulations, and topical files which pertain to long-term fiscal, regulatory, or control operations. Examples of records with short-term or limited administrative values are routine requests for information, transitory correspondence on matters of short-term interest, and convenience files maintained for an individual employee's use.[6]

Fiscal value

A record has fiscal value "if it pertains to the receipt, transfer, payment, adjustment, or encumbrance of funds, or if it is required for an audit."[5] Records that show routine financial transactions usually have limited value after audit. Those that document the evolution and implementation of fiscal policies usually have long-term value.

Legal value

A record possesses legal value "if it documents a legal right or obligation of a citizen or of the office or of the [local government] ... It will lose value at the point in time when the legal right ceases, or ceases to be enforceable under current law."[8] Records with legal value include legal decisions and opinions; documents embodying legal agreements, such as leases, titles, and contracts; and evidence of actions in particular cases, such as claims papers and legal dockets.

Appraising Records: Secondary Values

The "secondary" values of records are their importance for purposes beyond those for which they were originally created. It is helpful to distinguish two types of secondary values:

Evidential value

This value refers to the significance of the information a record provides on the government office and function that produced it. Records with a high degree of evidential value document the "organization, functions, policies, decisions, procedures, operations, or other activities" of government and "reflect decisions of organizations, programs, policies, and procedures ... and document supervisory and management activities and work processes."[9]

Informational value

Informational value depends on the degree of information in the records on "persons, places, subjects, and the like with which public agencies deal." This value is determined through analysis of the uniqueness of the records, the importance of its contents, the availability elsewhere of the information it contains, and the usefulness of the information for ongoing and potential research purposes.[10]

Archival Records

Those records with sufficient primary and/or secondary value to warrant their permanent retention are called archival records or simply archives. There is no easy way to identify all the archival records that a local government may have. Identification of these records "is fundamentally a search for possible cultural values to posterity. Does the records series provide valuable information on persons, events, or subjects? Does [it] provide valuable information on the key operations of a significant municipal office?"[11] The accompanying box provides additional informal guidelines for identifying archival records. These records deserve special care and preservation because of their importance to the government itself and to researchers. Their management is discussed in Chapter IX.

**Which Records are Archival?
Some General Guidelines**

Which local government records are archival and therefore worthy of permanent preservation? There is no simple answer to the question, but the appraisal process, described in this chapter, can be expected to identify many classes of archival records. State records retention and disposition schedules usually list records required to be retained permanently.

The guidelines below describe some general categories of records that are archival. They are provided for general assistance only and must be adjusted to meet particular circumstances. These guidelines draw on three sources which can provide further assistance: Maynard Brichford, *Archives and Manuscripts: Appraisal and Accessioning* (Chicago, 1977); H.G. Jones, *Local Government Records: An Introduction to Their Management, Preservation, and Use* (Nashville, 1980), especially Chapter VIII; and National Archives and Records Service, *Disposition of Federal Records* (Washington, 1981), especially Table 4, pp. 23-25, which is the source for much of this material.

•*Earliest local government records.* In the earliest years of local government operations, records were created in much smaller quantities than they are today. Many of these earliest records have disappeared through fire, flood, and general neglect. Therefore, it is often advisable to retain early records, even though their informational content may be limited, to show the functioning of government.

•*Minutes of governing bodies, boards, and commissions.* Minutes are usually the single most important records series in a local government. They document substantive policy and procedural decisions in almost all areas of importance to local government operations.

•*General subject files documenting substantive programs.* Reports, significant correspondence and internal memoranda, budget estimates and justifications, and other records documenting substantive programs, particularly those created by the leaders of government, are often worth retaining. These records document the evolution of major policies and programs and may also contain information on the community and its people.

•*Selected case files.* Many local government records are created in the form of case or project files. These may include correspondence, memoranda, reports, and other materials on specific actions, events, people, places, projects, or other topics. Especially important are those which document cases that established precedents, resulted in extended public controversy or litigation, or that clearly document the local government's typical approaches and procedures.

•*Analytical studies.* Analytical research studies and reports prepared by the local government or outside consultants can provide important information on outstanding problems and issues and on the plans developed to meet them.

•*Legal opinions.* Memoranda prepared by the local government's counsel or other officials, or opinions received from state authorities that concern interpretations of existing laws and regulations, are usually worthy of retention.

- *Evaluations of governmental operations.* Fiscal and program audits and studies made to determine the effectiveness of government programs and internal administrative arrangements can be very important. Particularly significant are those evaluations which recommend or result in changes in policy or procedures.
- *Formal directives, procedural issuances, and operating manuals.* These records document and show changes in the local government's policies and procedures and are invaluable in showing how government programs actually operated.
- *Public relations materials.* These include speeches, addresses, interview transcripts, news releases, and other materials distributed to the public on government programs or issues.
- *Publications.* At least one copy of all formal government publications should be retained for future reference. These include studies prepared by outside advisors or consultants, published reports, and brochures, flyers, and pamphlets.
- *Visual, audio, and graphic materials.* Government-produced photographs, sound and video recordings, architectural drawings, and other similar materials that cover significant subject matter should usually be retained.
- *Selected records with detailed information on individuals.* Because local government is closed to the people, many of the records it creates or assembles have detailed information on individuals. In many cases, these records have considerable legal significance as well as usefulness for a variety of historical and demographic research. These include: birth, death, and marriage records; records concerning orphans, apprentices, and other disadvantaged people participating in government welfare programs; police, court, jail, and other justice system records; school records; and military service records. Because of the personal nature of the information they contain, these records may present difficult issues regarding access.
- *Records with information on land and physical development of the area served by local government.* Another large category of valuable records are those that document land ownership and transfer and that show physical changes and development of the community. These include: deeds and other property records, recording property transfer and ownership; highway and transportation records that document development of the transportation network; and original maps, particularly those that document legal boundaries and subdivisions.

Retention and Disposition: Implementation

Retention of records as long as needed — but no longer — should be a tenet of local government records management. All employees including top elected or appointed officials, should recognize and acknowledge this responsibility. The records management officer should coordinate retention and disposition activities, and, working with agency or officer personnel, should review, refine, and update records schedules and disposition authorizations to keep them current. This will entail keeping up with changing state records retention and disposition requirements as well as with the local government's own need for records to be retained. Newly created series must be appraised and assigned retention periods as soon as possible after they come into existence.

Attention to scheduling and disposition should be tied to other aspects of records management. For instance, filing systems should include provision for retirement of inactive files and for their eventual disposition. Requests for new filing equipment should not be approved unless the requesting office is complying with existing schedules or other disposition authorizations. "Review of file equipment authorizations," notes one records manual, "is more of a records management function than a supply function."[12] Systematic periodic disposition is essential to the effective management of inactive records, discussed in Chapter VI. Records retention and disposition plans should be in place to make sure that records are not being kept longer than needed and that information retention needs are clear before planning micrographics or automated systems.

Obsolete records, which have outlived their established retention periods, should be culled periodically, for instance once a year or after each state audit, and destroyed. They should not be allowed to build into a storage problem. The records management officer is usually the logical choice to coordinate or carry out the actual disposal of the records. The means of disposal are usually up to the local government unless state requirements specify otherwise. One important consideration here is to protect the confidentiality of any sensitive information in the records by making sure that such records are destroyed without this information being disclosed. Some local governments turn obsolete records into revenue by selling them to paper recycling firms, with appropriate safeguards to protect confidential information. This approach provides a bonus to good records management.

The records management officer, or other official who carries out disposition, should keep a listing of records that are destroyed. Records disposition should be described in reports to the local government's chief executive officer or legislature. These reports should note: (1) the quantity of records disposed of; (2) resulting savings in terms of the replacement cost of filing cabinets and other records storage equipment released; (3) the value of the office and storage spaced released for reuse; and (4) other benefits, including the elimination of staff time required to service and sort through unneeded records, elimination of fire hazards, and better overall records administration.

Notes

1. Montgomery County, Ohio, Microfilming and Records Center, *Annual Report* (Dayton, 1984), 17.

2. T.R. Schellenberg, *Modern Archives: Principles and Techniques* (Chicago, 1956), 36.

3. William L. Rofes, ed., "A Basic Glossary For Archivists, Manuscript Curators, and Records Managers," *American Archivist*, 37 (July, 1974), 421.

4. *Ibid.*, 417.

5. Massachusetts Secretary of State, Division of Archives, *Municipal Records Manual* (Boston, 1983), "Introduction."

6. National Archives and Records Service, *Disposition of Federal Records* (Washington, 1981), 18-19.

7. David Levine, ed., *Local Government Records Handbook* (Columbus, 1984), 9.

8. Massachusetts Secretary of State, *Municipal Records Manual*, "Introduction."

9. Rofes, ed., "Basic Glossary," 422; Maynard E. Brichford, *Archives and Manuscripts: Appraisal and Accessioning* (Chicago, 1977), 5.

10. Rofes, ed., "Basic Glossary," 424; Brichford, *Appraisal and Accessioning*, 5.

11. Massachusetts Secretary of State, *Municipal Records Manual*, "Introduction."

12. National Archives and Records Service, *Disposition of Federal Records*, 58.

5
Organizing and Controlling Active Records

The Need to Get Organized

Local governments create records for several purposes: to record information, to document transactions, to communicate thought, and to provide lasting evidence of events. In order for records to serve these purposes, however, three goals must be met. First, the records must actually contain enough information to guide government and to document governmental actions. Second, the information must be presented clearly and intelligibly. And, third, the records must be methodically organized so that their information can be found when it is needed. This chapter discusses several ways to meet these three goals. The suggestions can be used by any local government to get its records organized.

Correspondence Management

Correspondence — letters to and from government and memoranda between people within the government — comprises a sizeable proportion of any local government's total records. A helpful way of conveying information, correspondence is costly to produce and even costlier to maintain. For instance, the average business letter costs over $8 to produce and mail.[1] Local governments may spend less, but the costs are still significant and, of course, filing and storage require additional outlays. Effective correspondence control should begin at the time of creation and aim to eliminate much of the paperwork and associated storage and management costs. Correspondence management includes these approaches:

- Create letters and memos only when needed to convey information or to create a tangible record. Otherwise, rely on face-to-face conversations or the telephone.
- Use preprinted form letters, stock paragraphs, and word processing equipment whenever possible to cut down on redundant typing.
- Plan correspondence carefully to keep the reader's information needs in mind. Organize the material logically, include only what is necessary, and make sure the writing is concise, clear, and to the point.
- Produce only needed copies to prevent unnecessary handling and cut down on file build up.
- Carefully annotate file copies where necessary to ensure speedy and accurate filing.

Reports Control

Reports summarize and convey information needed by program managers and by other officials who use the information to carry out their work, and by auditors, state and federal officials, and the general public. Reports should be well organized, clearly presented, and tailored to the needs of their intended audience. Many local government reports are prescribed by state or federal requirements, but local government officials can choose which additional reports to create and how to create them. Having too few reports will mean that officials and the public will have too little information. Having too many reports will mean that important information will be scattered and difficult to locate and integrate.

A reports control program should encourage production of only necessary reports, ensure that they are well designed and convey appropriate information, and eliminate all unnecessary reports. In analyzing and determining the continuing need for reports, it is helpful to ask:

Organizing and Controlling Active Records 55

Are you feeling the squeeze of accumulated paperwork?

Are your filing cabinets overflowing?

Are you running out of valuable work space?

Are your records getting to be too expensive in terms of staff time or lost records?

Albany County Hall of Records offers cost-efficient, effective, and comprehensive records management to County and City agencies.

- Advisory Services
- Off-site Storage
- Reference and Retrieval Services
- Confidential Legal Destruction
- Micrographics
- Vital Records Protection
- Courier Service

Let us work with you to establish a dependable program based on your specific needs.

FOR INFORMATION, PLEASE CONTACT:

Albany County
Hall *of* RECORDS
Albany County Clerk

250 South Pearl Street
Albany, New York 12202
447-4500

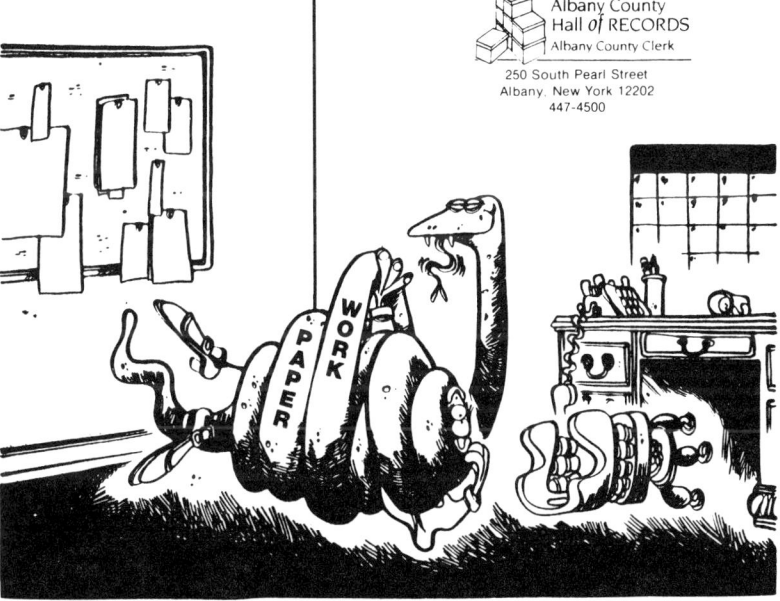

Fig. 5.1 Just about every local government office has a paperwork monster that needs taming. Records programs can use touches of humor to get attention for records management needs and services. (Albany County, NY, Hall of Records)

• Why is the report created? What administrative, legal, or other need does it serve? What would happen if it were discontinued?
• How important is the information in the report? Who uses it, and for what purposes?
• How frequently is it prepared? Should it be prepared more frequently? Less frequently?
• Is the information in the report available elsewhere? Does it overlap with information in other reports?
• How many copies are made, and where are they filed?
• How well is the report organized? Could its information be presented in a better way?

Forms Management

Forms are the most common records in many local government offices. They are used to communicate information in a "methodical, standardized, and repetitive way" and to "guide the flow of work through an office or agency and facilitate the rapid collection and transmittal of information in compact form."[2] Forms are useful information workhorses but they can also create problems. Local governments may create too many forms, use forms that require unnecessary or excessive information, or rely on forms that are poorly designed, confusing, or lack clear instructions. Forms are expensive to print — and processing, storing, and handling costs can be as much as *twenty* times the printing costs![3] It's easy to see why forms management must be a part of the attack on the paper mountain in local government offices. Forms management has the dual goals of speeding information flow and cutting costs. It should:

• Analyze the informational content and use of existing forms in relation to their cost. Discontinue forms that no longer serve a useful purpose.
• Bring together and consolidate forms with substantially the same informational content or function.
• Eliminate unneeded information on forms.

- Eliminate unnecessary extra copies of forms to cut down on paperwork handling and storage costs.
- Monitor the use of forms to continually evaluate their effectiveness.
- Design new forms as needed to achieve maximum efficiency and usefulness.
- Ensure that all forms have established retention periods.
- Identify the most economical method of printing forms, coordinate printing, and oversee inventory control and reprinting.

Filing Systems

Well-organized filing systems are effective weapons in the war to control local government paperwork. A filing system is a method of organizing records by placing them in predetermined locations according to an overall classification scheme. The system features hierarchical breakdowns — major subject categories are subdivided into successive levels of subordinate topics. The purpose of any filing system is to make it easier to rapidly retrieve information when needed. With the cost of a misfiled records around $80, it is apparent that filing systems save money as well as time.[4] Standardized filing systems have these advantages:[5]

- Integrity and continuity of records. Records are organized according to a single, standard, and continuing approach, no matter who is responsible for the function or who does the filing.
- Efficiency of personnel. File clerks, secretaries, and other personnel who file and retrieve records all operate under the same system, file the same way, and can retrieve records the same way.
- Better communication. A common approach to filing makes it easier for the users and keepers of records to work together in retrieving and using information.
- Aid to audit, research, and other uses. A well-organized system presents all the records in a clear, straightforward way

that also constitutes evidence of how the functions evolved, how the records were built up, and how each individual record relates to others.

Four Approaches to Files Arrangement

The four most common filing methods are alphabetical, numeric, alphanumeric, and chronological. An *alphabetical* system maintains material in alphabetical order by the name of the subject. It is the most common application for files on individuals, companies, organizations, projects, and other subjects. The system is easy to set up and learn, simple to update, flexible, expandable, and virtually self-indexing. Its usefulness may be limited, however, with large files having many duplicate or similar names. A *numeric* system is well suited to records that are pre-numbered, such as cancelled checks, invoices, vouchers, and licenses, or in which a number is assigned to records according to a pre-arranged scheme. An *alphanumeric* system involves classification of records by codes, either alphabetical, numerical, or in combinations. A *chronological* system, as the name implies, puts records in order by date. Each of the four filing methods may be appropriate for local government records. The choice depends on the nature of the records, rate of file growth, and, most important, how users retrieve and use records from the file.

Types of Files

Filing systems vary greatly from one local government to the next, but most are constructed around *series* of records, as discussed in Chapter IV. Some of the more common types are:[6]

• *Case or project files.* A case file is a folder or other file unit that "contains material relating to a specific action, transaction, event, person, place, [or] project." The records may cover many aspects of a case or project but are maintained together as an integral unit. The files "document a transaction or relationship from beginning to end"; for example, a copy of a lease might begin a file, and the relinquishment of the lease may close it.[7] Examples of these types of files include personnel files, contract files, legal files, and project files relating to an assigned task or problem.

• *Case working papers.* These are "short-lived correspondence and working papers accumulated in connection with specific case and project files," including background and working materials, data analyses and summaries, and "drafts and other preliminary or intermediate papers leading to final results or findings."

• *Subject files.* A broad category of files are those that contain information on "policies, procedures, and general administrative matters." These files are often called "correspondence files," "general files," "central files," or simply "subject files." Under this scheme, files are established in line with the functions of local government offices. All the information on a particular subject is grouped in one place, with cross references to guide the user to related topics or names.

• *Transitory correspondence files.* These files include "... correspondence and other papers of short-term interest ... [that] involve routine transactions and do not contain information of continuing reference value." Examples are transmittal letters and forms, requests for routine information, communications to correct records, and "other documents not requiring any action by the receiving office." In most cases, these materials should be assigned a relatively short minimum retention period.

• *Technical reference files.* These files include technical reports, periodicals, catalogs, manuals, and other materials assembled and retained for reference purposes. Some of this material may not actually be official record material, depending on the legal definition in effect, but it "has a direct relationship to the work of the office and is needed for future reference."

• *Convenience files.* These are extra copies of correspondence, forms, and other papers kept solely for convenience of reference. Examples include chronological files, suspense or "tickler" files, and duplicate working files.

Fig. 5.2 Orderly filing of records is essential to control, store, and retrieve the growing volume of information in local government offices. Uniform, systematic filing systems provide the basis for the order that is needed. (Montgomery County, Ohio, Microfilming and Records Center)

Filing Systems: Canons of Good Practice

No matter what the type of the filing system, success depends on a number of factors:

• *Everyone must understand, accept, and use the system.* If a filing system is to succeed, everyone from top management on down must support, endorse, and use it. Alternative or parallel systems must be discouraged. Training sessions are useful when a system is established and when new employees are hired, and a filing handbook that explains and describes the system is very helpful.

• *"Files maintenance begins when the record is produced in your office or received from someone else."*[8] Sound filing systems are assisted by sound records management practices throughout government, and *vice versa*. For instance, one way to promote streamlined filing systems is to prevent unnecessary copies from getting into the files in the first place. This is achieved through limiting the number of extra copies produced and through systematic management and control of correspondence, memoranda, reports, and forms.

•*"Retention awareness" is an essential element when setting up a filing system.*[9] A sound filing system should relate closely to the local government's retention and disposition schedules. Retention and disposition considerations should be taken into account when the system is planned so that records can be easily transferred from active to inactive storage. For instance, transitory correspondence should be filed separately from general subject files since their retention periods will almost surely differ. Even within files, it may help to divide papers of short-term retention from those that need to be kept longer, to eliminate having to sort through all the papers in the file later on. Filing systems should include provision for periodic file breaks or cutoffs — physically separating those files that are inactive or closed from those that are active and open. Inactive records can then be transferred to an inactive records storage facility and obsolete records may be removed and destroyed in accordance with approved schedules. This weeding process can also be aided by noting the closing date on the tabs or front panels of case folders.

•*Physical maintenance is important.* Neatness and orderliness are essential to good files. Among recommended practices are the following: (1) label file drawers or doors to indicate files or subjects; (2) use files with uniform folder tabs; (3) use folder guides to divide the files; (4) do not overload files — when a folder is full, add a second one with the same designation or subdivide by creating new file designations; (5) be consistent in preparing records for filing by removing rubber bands, paper clips, pins, etc., carefully checking for completeness and proper filing location, and discarding routing slips, envelopes, and other unnecessary material; (6) keep papers straight—do not let them extend beyond the edges of the folders; (7) avoid cluttering files with bulky items — file these elsewhere and cross-reference; and (8) do not overcrowd the files — a good rule of thumb is to allow at least four inches in each active drawer to permit working space.[10]

•*File station locations should be carefully selected.* The physical location of the files is important. For a small operation, centralization may be the best approach. This brings the records together in one location, eliminates the need for duplicate files and equipment, and ensures that all staff are familiar with the entire filing operation. But for a larger office or agency, decentralized files and multiple filing stations will be necessary because of the quantity of the records and the need for close proximity to the offices that create and use them.

Freedom of Information.

The need to conform to state Freedom of Information and personal privacy laws shapes strategies for organizing and controlling records. These laws attempt to balance the right of public access to records against a responsibility to maintain the confidentiality of sensitive information. The laws usually prescribe conditions under which records are to be accessible or else indicate the conditions under which they may be withheld or closed. These laws may have at least three effects on government records systems and programs:

•Access and privacy considerations must be taken into account when establishing records-keeping systems for instance, special provisions need to be built into filing systems if selected documents or files are to be restricted or withheld from public inspection.

•Some state laws require compilation of subject-matter lists of records to guide Freedom of Information requests. Creation and maintenance of such a list might be tied to the records inventory, to the creation of file lists or indexes to filing systems, or to records retention and disposition schedules.

•Many of the state laws require local governments to designate a records access officer. This may be a logical assignment for the records management officer, in conjunction with his or her other records-related duties. If not, the records access officer needs to work closely with the records management officer.

Vital Records

"Vital" records are those essential to the continuing operation of the government. They contain the information that would be needed to resume and continue operation of the government after a major disaster, such as a fire or flood, to protect the legal and financial interests of the government, and to preserve the rights of the people. Vital records may include: minutes, fiscal and accounting records, tax rolls, franchises, maps and surveys that document legal boundaries, deeds, highway and street designations, payrolls, and other essential employee records, and insurance policies.

These essential records need a high level of security and protection from fire, theft, and other threats. In fact, some states require special protection for vital records such as storage in approved records vaults or safes. The state agencies listed in Appendix I can provide information in this area. Another approach, sometimes called "duplication and dispersal," involves making a microfilm or other copy of the records and placing the copy at a safe location away from the originals. This approach makes it highly unlikely that both copies of the records would be destroyed in a single disaster. Local governments should also develop disaster response plans for salvaging and restoring records that are damaged by fire or flood.

Notes

1. Figure from Dartnell Institute of Business Research in *Office Systems '84*, I (November, 1984), 10.
2. *Illinois Local Records Management Handbook* (Springfield, 1984), 11.
3. *Ibid.*, 11.
4. Giovanna B. Seguin and Carrie Miller Townley, *An Introduction to Filing Systems* (Prairie Village, KS, 1981), VI.

5. National Archives and Records Service, *Subject Filing* (Washington, n.d.), 2.

6. This section follows closely City of Portland, Oregon, *Records Manual*, prepared by Stanley Parr *et al.* (Rev. ed., Portland, 1980), 6-8. Quotations in this section are from this source unless otherwise noted.

7. National Archives and Records Service, *Case Filing,* (Washington, n.d.), 1.

8. Michael J. Fox and Kathleen A. McDonough, *Wisconsin Municipal Records Manual* (Madison, 1980), 8.

9. Seguin and Townley, *Introduction to Filing Systems,* 2.

10. City of Portland, *Records Manual,* 18-19.

6
Management of Inactive Records

Separate Management

You can save time and money by consolidating inactive records in one place under the oversight of one person. As explained in Chapter IV, records enter their inactive phase after serving the immediate purposes of their creation. One informal rule says records referred to less than once per month per file drawer have become inactive. They are still needed occasionally for government business but they need not be retained in their offices of origin. They can, and should, be sent to a secure storage facility, or records center, to await their final destiny: outright destruction for the vast majority, after they reach their established retention periods, or permanent preservation as part of an archival program.

The records center serves as a way-station in the life cycle of records. "Orderliness, compactness, and security form the trinity of records center philosophy," notes one authority. "Its prime objective is the elimination of the need for 'dumping areas' by providing properly designed, equipped, and staffed space where records can be housed and serviced more efficiently and economically than they can be if kept in prime office areas or forgotten storerooms and other hiding places."[1]

Advantages of An Inactive Records Program

An inactive records program affords several benefits:
•*Fewer records held in active office areas.* Moving records into an inactive records facility as they reach their inactive phase, frees expensive office space and equipment for newer records.

Fig. 6.1 Standard-sized, well-labeled records cartons in order on steel shelving are hallmarks of an efficient local government records storage center. Coordination by the government's records management officer and the use of specified forms and procedures for use of the records center will help ensure its success as part of the records program. (Montgomery County, Ohio, Microfilming and Records Center)

• *Better use of available space.* Records can be concentrated and stored more compactly in a records facility than in active office areas. For instance, records stored in standard file cabinets in offices require one square foot of floor space per cubic foot of records. When they are stored in standard records cartons on shelves in a records center, the ratio can increase to five cubic feet of records to each square foot of floor space.[2]

• *Cost savings.* Space costs in an inactive records facility are usually less than in active offices. Furthermore, once records are transferred to cartons for storage at the records center, filing cabinets and other records storage equipment can be freed for reuse, making purchase of new equipment unnecessary. The cost avoidance and costs savings will be considerable over time. According to one estimate, it costs *twelve times* as much to keep records in an office file as an inactive records center.[3]

•*Easier, faster records retrieval.* Records can be retrieved faster and easier from a records center than from overcrowded office files or attics, basements, or disorganized storerooms, because they are stored systematically and their shelf location is carefully noted at the time of transfer.

•*Better control.* It is easier to assert and maintain intellectual and physical control over records in a records center than over records scattered through government offices and storage areas.

•*Security.* Records in a secure facility are protected from theft, fire, flood, and other natural disasters, and from unwarranted destruction.

•*Systematic legal disposition.* An inactive records program includes built-in procedures and controls to ensure the orderly, periodic disposition of records after they reach their established retention periods.

Program Coordination

An inactive records program needs coordination if it is to succeed. An uncoordinated effort with an unmonitored records storage center, freely accessible to everyone, will usually not work. Lack of coordination is likely to cause problems:

•Some departments will continue to hold inactive records in their offices, just as they have always done.

•Some offices will set up their own, proprietary storage areas or stake out a claim to part of the records center.

•Records will be sent to the records center without adequate listings or controls and without specified retention periods.

•In a few years, the center will be full of disorganized and mostly unidentified records.

An inactive program will run smoothly, however, if coordinating responsibility is assigned to the records management officer or some other individual. This person should:

• Use the local government's initial records inventory to estimate the needed size of the records center facility, including growth for several years in the future.
• Plan the records center.
• Oversee and coordinate construction and/or outfitting of the records center.
• Operate the records center directly or through a records center manager and staff.
• Educate local government employees about the concept of inactive records and their management.
• Actively and continually encourage offices to use the records center for their inactive records.
• Develop forms and procedures for use by offices in transferring records to the center.
• Develop and apply controls to locate records within the records center and to retrieve records when needed.
• Retrieve records when requested by the originating office.
• In conjunction with records custodians, monitor retention periods of records in the records center and ensure destruction of records that have passed their established retention periods.
• See to it that archival records temporarily stored in the records center are transferred to the local government's archives at the appropriate time for permanent preservation.
• Periodically report on records center operations and on the overall inactive records program.

The Records Storage Center

A secure place to store records is essential for any inactive records program. The term "records center" may imply something larger and more elaborate than what is actually needed. A large government may need a warehouse with thousands of cubic feet of storage capacity. A small or intermediate-sized government, however, may need only a large, secure, properly outfitted room. Several factors need consideration when planning for a records center facility:

•*Size.* The center needs space for receiving and processing records and possibly for administrative office space and for reference use of the records. Most important, it needs storage space to accommodate future growth. The storage capacity needed will depend on: (1) the volume of inactive records; these figures should be available from the records inventory; (2) projected future growth; the rate-of-increase figures from the inventory will provide some assistance here; (3) the volume of movement *out* of the records center as retention periods expire and records are either destroyed or sent to the government's archives.

•*Location.* The records center should be in, or as near as possible to, the building where most local government employees work, and where, therefore, most records are generated and used. Location should be balanced against space and security requirements. In-house facilities are ideal if appropriate space is available, but often the best location will be a secure building in a low-rent area. If an off-site location is selected, it should include a dock for easy loading and unloading of records. Provision must be made for quick, easy retrieval of records when they are needed.

•*Security.* The facility must be secure, clean, and well maintained. Basement areas are not desirable because of likely humidity control problems and the risk of flooding in the event of high water or fire. To guard against unwarranted entry, the door to the stacks should be locked with only records center and security personnel having keys.

•*Floor strength.* The floor must be capable of bearing the full weight of the records, which will average around 30 lbs. per cubic foot.

•*Fire protection.* The records center should be constructed of fireproof materials and equipped with a fire detection and alarm system. It should also include a sprinkler or other fire suppression system.

•*Temperature and humidity controls.* Clean air and good ventilation are essential to protect the records from dust and dirt. Air conditioning is highly desirable. Both temperature and humidity should be kept in the moderate zone: temperatures of 65-75 degrees F, and relative humidity of 30-60 percent. The facility's controls must not allow rapid, extreme fluctuations in temperature and humidity, which can be very damaging to records. Special provisions may be needed for storing records on media such as microfilm and computer tapes.

•*Shelving.* Records centers should be equipped with steel shelving installed in such a way as to make maximum use of available floor space. Records storage facilities commonly use steel shelving that is 30" x 42" in dimension, with shelves approximately 13" apart vertically. Each of these shelves will accommodate six standard "records center cartons," with dimensions of 10" x 12" x 15". These shelves are also big enough to accept larger records such as rolled maps and architectural drawings.

•*Aisles.* Records facilities need aisles wide enough for comfortable passage of a person with a cart for hauling boxes. Aisle width of 30" to 36" is usually considered sufficient.

Program Management

Control of inactive records is a continuous responsibility. The records management officer or other person in charge of the inactive records program should develop forms and guidelines that explain the inactive records program and the procedures for transferring records to the inactive records storage facility. Listed below are some elements that should be included:

•*Periodic transfer of inactive records.* Files cutoff and transfer of inactive records to the records center should be standard operating procedures, as noted in the discussion of filing systems in Chapter V. Records should be transferred on a regular basis, such as once a year, rather than waiting until office files are full.

•*Custody.* A records center is essentially a temporary storehouse for records. The records management officer or other person in charge of the records center brings records into the facility, assigns shelf space to them, and has *physical* custody of the records while they are there. But *legal* custody in most cases remains with the originating office, which retains primary responsibility for the preservation of the records, for deciding who may see them, and for their ultimate disposition.

•*Transfer procedures.* The records center must not become a dumping ground for unwanted records, and the program itself needs careful controls and procedures governing transfer. The records management officer or records center manager should develop procedures for documenting transfer of records into the records center. Some local governments use computers for this purpose. More common is the use of a simple control form, usually called a "Records Center Transfer List." Offices fill out the form before transferring records to the records center. The form should provide at least the following information: (1) name of transferring office; (2) identity and inclusive dates of the records being transferred; (3) listing of boxes or volumes; and (4) the established retention period for the record. It is helpful to use a three-part form or to make two copies. One copy can then be used as a locator file to indicate where the records are stored in the records center. One can be filed in a "tickler file" according to the projected disposition date. The third can be returned to the originating office as documentation that the records have been received and placed in storage.

•*Internal control.* Incoming records should be assigned to available storage space by the records center manager as they are received from their offices. Cartons of records received from one department may in most cases be given shelf space alongside records from another office. The records center manager must, of course, keep track of the location of all records so that they can be retrieved when needed. One approach is to use a copy of the records transfer list as a locator file. Some local governments have begun using computers for this purpose.

•*Access and retrieval.* The originating office retains legal custody and therefore determines who may use the records, but the person in charge of the records center has responsibility for physical access to the records. This person must develop procedures for letting authorized personnel examine the records at the records center and/or for temporarily returning the records to the office of origin, or providing copies, when needed for use there.

•*Regular disposition.* When records are transferred to a records center, an assigned retention period should be indicated on the transfer list. Many records centers make it a rule not to accept records that do not have assigned retention periods. Records should be destroyed, or transferred to the archives, in accordance with the established retention period. It may be easiest to carry out disposition periodically, for instance once a year or after state audits. The records center manager should notify the office of origin, and secure their approval, before carrying out disposition. The disposition of the records should be documented through a notation on the records transfer list or in some other way.

Tracking and Reporting on Records Center Operations

A systematically administered inactive records program will save money and improve information control and retrieval. The records management officer or records center manager should carefully keep track of records center operations. He or she should periodically report on the inactive records program, including:

•Quantity of records received and stored, broken down according to department or office of origin.

•Number of reference requests handled.

•Volume of records legally destroyed.

•Estimates of cost avoidance and cost savings achieved through the services of the records center.

•Discussion of how records center operations contributed to information retrieval and use.

Notes

1. H.G. Jones, *Local Government Records: An Introduction to Their Management, Preservation, and Use* (Nashville, 1980), 59.
2. Wilmer O. Maedke, Mary F. Robek, and Gerald F. Brown, *Information and Records Management* (Encino, CA, 1981), 293.
3. State of Washington, Department of General Administration, Division of Archives and Records Management, *Local Government Records Workshop Handbook* (Olympia, n.d.), 22.

INSTRUCTIONS FOR THE PREPARATION OF RECORDS FOR TRANSFER (using the form on pages 74-75)

Packing Records

To streamline the packing process and to simplify future retrieval and disposal requirements, please observe the following rules in preparing records for transfer:

1. *Pack records upright in the storage boxes.* The boxes are so constructed that they will store letter size materials one way and legal size the other.
2. *Keep records in numerical, alphabetical or chronological order,* or as they are normally filed in cabinets.
3. *Fill box to capacity.* Do not over-pack. If a record is to be retained in the department temporarily, but is to be sent to the Records Center for "in filing" at a later date, sufficient space must be left in the appropriate carton to accommodate the item.
4. *Pack one records series to a box.* Series may be mixed only if required to fill a box.
5. *Pack records with the same retention period together* in one or more consecutive storage cartons. When records with a different retention period must be included to fill a carton, indicate the separation point clearly.
6. Place label, when required, on end of box without staples beneath hand hold.

City of Rochester - Records Transfer List
City Clerk/Records Management

Page _____ of _____

① DEPT:	① BUREAU:	② DIVISION	③
DATE	④ RECORDS APPROVED FOR MICROFILMING	⑤ DATE FILMED	⑥

FILING EQUIPMENT RELEASED
For Reuse ☐   Recycle ☐
Number of Legal Size Cabinets _____
Number of Letter Size Cabinets _____
Other (describe) _____

⑦ LOCATION _____

OFFICE AND STORAGE SPACE RELEASED ⑧
Office _____ sq. Ft.
Storage _____ sq. Ft.
Formula: One 4 drawer cabinet = 6.7 sq. ft.

BOX NO. ⑨	RECORDS TITLE ⑩	YEARS COVERED ⑪	ACCESS CODE ⑫	RRDS AND ITEM NO. ⑬	DESTRUCT DATE ⑭	DATE DESTROYED ⑮	BIN NUMBER ⑯

Fig. 6.2. A simple but workable form should be developed for listing records transferred to a local government's inactive records center. The sample form above, developed by the City of Rochester's Records Management Program, includes provision for listing records title, inclusive years, item number on records retention and dispo-

BOX NO. ⑨	RECORDS TITLE ⑩	YEARS COVERED ⑪	ACCESS CODE ⑫	RRDS AND ITEM NO. ⑬	DESTRUCT DATE ⑭	DATE DE-STROYED ⑮	BIN NUMBER ⑯

⑰ DEPT. SIGNATURE: _____ TITLE: _____ DATE: _____

RECORDS RECEIVED BY: _____ DATE: _____

Revised 10/1981

sition schedules, location within the records center, and information on eventual disposition. From the Rochester Records Managment Program, Records Manual *(Rochester, 1984)*

7. *Number each box consecutively in the appropriate section on the box or label.* Start a new series for each shipment of a different year. Do not put any other marks or labels, other than those provided, on the box.

Completing Records Transfer Lists

When boxes of records are prepared for storage at the Records Center, a City of Rochester Records Transfer List must be completed by the user for *each series* of records and each shipment. Limit one records series per transfer list. The transfer lists must be typed and completed in the following manner:

SECTION	DIRECTIONS
1-3	*Dept., Bureau Division* - Complete all boxes that are appropriate for your office.
4	*Date* - Enter date records are packed or transfer list is prepared.
5	*Records Approved for Microfilming* - Complete only if previous approval has been given by authorized department personnel and Records Management by placing a "yes" in this box.
6	*Date Filmed* - For Records Management Use.
7	*Filing Equipment released* - Check appropriate statement as it applies to status of filing equipment from which records are removed. Select appropriate cabinet size and enter the total emptied as it applies to each shipment of records. For "Other," describe type of equipment released, such as map cabinet, lateral file, shelving units, etc. Location - Give location of file equipment such as building and room number or office area.
8	*Office and Storage Space Released* - Using formula given in this section, determine office space freed when entire cabinet(s) is/are emptied and removed from office. Use same formula for space other then office area released and enter in "storage" line.
9	*Box Number* - The box number must correspond to the number penciled on the box as assigned by person filling box.
10	*Records Title* - Use the same title for the record it is to be stored under and later refered to when requesting records retrieval. Be explicit and enter as much information as necessary so that there is no doubt as to what the records are.
11	*Years Covered* - List the year(s), also months and date if applicable, of the particular records packed in box. For fiscal year records, list of FY 1979-80, for example.

Management of Inactive Records

12 *Access Code* - For Records Management Use.

13 *R.R.D.S. and Item number* - R.R.D.S. refers to the appropriate Records Retention and Disposition Schedule such as 11-city-1. Item number refers to the number under which the records on the transfer list fall in the retention schedule. Enter both in this column opposite records title.

14 *Destruct Date* - Enter date that records are eligible for destruction as calculated from "Disposable after being retained" column from appropriate retention schedule. Calendar year records are disposed of in January and fiscal year records in July. In determining destruction date, use the formula current year of records plus the required retention period. For Archival records, enter Archival-permanent in this section.

15 *Date Destroyed* - For Records Management use.

16 *Bin Number* - For Records Management Use

17 *Dept. Signature* - Either the department head or departmental records coordinator should complete this line with signature, title, and date.

18 *Records Received By* - For Records Management use.

A Records Program That Works: Montgomery County Ohio

The Montgomery County, Ohio, records program, one of the best in the nation and winner of the Association of Records Managers and Administrators' Olsten Award for Excellence in Records Management, is a success story that can serve as an inspiration and a model for other local governments.

A few years ago, the County, a large metropolitan area with Dayton as its county seat, had serious records problems: inactive records consumed valuable space in county buildings; some offices carelessly dumped old records; microfilming applications were poorly planned and ineffective; and the accumulation of records continued each year. In 1979, the County's elected officials confronted the problem by establishing a records management program and appointing Stephen E. Haller as records manager. He has broad responsibilities, including general records management assistance and consulting for all county agencies, supervision of micrographics operations, oversight of computer output microfilming, management of the county records center, and coordination of the county's word processing network. He makes sure these responsibilities work in tandem toward the goal of improved records management.

Aggressive implementation of state-approved records retention and disposition schedules assists in the orderly destruction of Montogomery County's valueless records. Inactive records are transferred to the county records center, which now holds nearly 22,000 cubic feet of material from 40 county offices and agencies. The center's mission is service, and it handles nearly 30,000 reference requests per year. Over 3,000 cubic feet of valueless on microfilmed records are destroyed each year.

Microfilm is another mainstay of the program. The county's microfilm office produces consistently high quality film. In most cases, the original records are destroyed after filming, resulting in space and cost savings. The program produces over eight million document images annually, involving several dozen applications from the County Auditor, Sheriff, Treasurer, Welfare Department, and other agencies.

Service and communication throughout county government are also important tenets of the Montgomery program. The Records Manager prepares a detailed plan for each year's microfilming operations and other aspects of records management and submits quarterly and annual reports. He works closely with department heads on specific records problems and conducts training on records systems and procedures. There is a 20-minute slide presentation on the microfilming and records center operations.

The program is a significant money saver for the county. "Through the judicious and regular use of records management tools, considerable performance improvements have been realized," notes Haller. "We have been able to manage and control the paperwork monster in an organized, professional manner." A careful analysis of cost avoidance and cost savings from the microfilming and records center operations alone resulted in an annual savings estimate of $500,000 after operating costs. Records will occupy less than three percent of the space in a newly contstructed county-city justice center.

The county record center also houses many of the county's archival records. Ohio has a network of regional historical records repositories and the Montgomery County program cooperates with it. Records from discontinued offices or functions are transferred to the Ohio Historical Society for preservation at its network center at Wright State University in Dayton.

Montgomery County is larger than many local governments, but its program has characteristics that can lead to success anywhere: support from the legislative body, cooperation from individual offices, an able records officer, persistent use of records retention and disposition schedules to continually dispose of obsolete records, an inactive records center, and appropriate use of microfilming and other technology to produce significant savings.

For more information on the Montgomery County program, contact County Records Manager, Stephen E. Haller, 451 West Third Street, Dayton, Ohio 45422.

7
Micrographics and Local Government Records Management

Microfilm: An Information Management Tool

Local governments need all the allies they can find in the struggle with paperwork, and microfilming is one of the best! Microfilming is the photographic process of creating miniaturized images of records on film. It concentrates information in a compact, durable, and easy-to-use form which, through the use of microfilm readers and reader-printers, can be projected back to original size when needed. Film produced to acceptable quality standards will stand the test of time. And, when state legal requirements are met, the original copies of many records can be destroyed and the microfilm copies substituted. A well-planned, systematic microfilming program can have several benefits, including:

•*Information handling and retrieval.* Microfilm captures and holds large quantities of information in a form that is easier to handle and manipulate than the corresponding paper records. The information is concentrated and can be located close to where the user needs it.

•*Information sharing and dissemination.* Multiple copies of microfilm can be sent wherever needed so that people can use the same information in more than one location at the same time.

•*Space savings.* Microfilm takes up only about 2 percent of the storage space required for corresponding paper records, making for dramatic space savings.

Fig. 7.1 Microfilming transforms information from a bulky format to a compact one. When carried out to appropriate technical standards, it is an excellent information tool for local governments. (Tennessee State Library and Archives)

- *File integrity.* Microfilming freezes information in a fixed order, preventing loss of information through lost or misplaced files or documents.
- *Security.* Duplicate copies of microfilm can be stored away from the original records and away from the original (camera-produced) microfilm, ensuring survival of the information even if the original records or original film are damaged or destroyed.
- *Preservation.* Microfilm produced and stored to appropriate standards is a reliable medium for preserving information. It can also directly contribute to the preservation of the records themselves by permitting them to be withdrawn from use and the microfilm copy substituted in their place.
- *Cost benefits.* A systematic microfilm program can result in significant savings and cost avoidance from reduced storage space, accelerated information retrieval, efficient information dissemination, and improved file security.

Microfilming: Limitations and Drawbacks

Microfilm also has some limitations and drawbacks, however, particularly if it is not planned as an integral part of a total records management strategy:

- *Not a substitute for good records management.* Microfilming will not solve accumulated records problems or overcome bad records handling practices such as disorganized files or unnecessary storage of inactive records in active office areas. It may, in fact, perpetuate such problems by freezing the information in its disorganized state.
- *Expense.* Microfilming is costly, whether carried out in-house or through a service agency. Expenses can outweigh cost benefits in the absence of proper planning.
- *Technical challenges.* Microfilming quality standards must be observed or the film may be hard to read or deteriorate over time.
- *Need for viewer equipment.* Readers and/or reader-printers

are required for reading the film and for making paper prints.

•*User resistance.* Some people dislike having to use microfilm because it can cause visual discomfort and fatigue.

Planning for Microfilming

Microfilm can be a helpful ally but its use must be planned to contribute to broader records management goals. There are three good ways to begin planning for microfilming. The first is to check with the state archival or records office listed in Appendix I for information on technical requirements and procedures for disposal or original records after filming. The second is to contact other local governments in your region that have already developed microfilming programs and can provide practical advice. The third is to check the publications mentioned later in this chapter and in Chapter X.

With a basic grounding in microfilming techniques, you can then turn to analysis of the records being considered for filming. The information in the inventory described in Chapter III should be very helpful here. A number of factors need consideration:

•*Microfilming goals.* What are the goals of microfilming: Preservation of the information in the records? Dissemination of the information? Destruction of the original records after filming? A combination of these objectives? How will the microfilming effort fit in with and contribute to overall records management goals? Could the objectives of microfilming be accomplished as well, or better, in other ways, such as more systematic management of inactive records or disposition of obsolete records?

•*Informational content and use.* Is the information in the records valuable enough to justify reproduction on film? Who uses the records now, and who would use the microfilm, for what purposes, how frequently, and in what locations?

•*Retention period.* How long must the original records be kept? Have retention and disposition schedules been developed, approved, adopted, and utilized? It is usually more cost effective to retain records with retention periods of 12-15 years or less than it is to microfilm them.

•*Quantity.* How voluminous are the records? Are new files or items still being added? Usually, important records with high volume and long retention periods are the best candidates for microfilming.

•*Physical characteristics.* What is the size, shape, and condition of the records? Are they faded or do they contain faint handwriting or have other drawbacks that will make them difficult to capture on film? How much variation is there from item to item?

•*Preparation.* Are the records organized in their original order or in some other logical fashion so that their information can be located on the film, or will they require reorganization before filming? How much time and effort will be required to unfold documents, remove clips, staples, rubber bands, and other fasteners, and to prepare appropriate identification targets?

•*Legal requirements.* What state statutory provisions govern the reproduction of local government records? State laws may prescribe minimum quality standards and microfilm identification provisions that must be followed for the film to be substituted for the original records in court proceedings and for other purposes. They may also establish requirements for disposal of the original records after filming.

•*Film in-house or use a service bureau?* The choice between developing an in-house capacity and contracting with a microfilm service bureau may be the most difficult one to make. Local governments with a continuing need to film sizeable quantities of records may decide to purchase equipment, hire or train staff, develop the technical expertise needed to produce quality film, and carry out their own work. On the other hand, a reliable service agency with a professional staff and a reputation for quality work may be the best choice if quantities are limited, the need is intermittent rather than continuing, the filming application entails special equipment or challenges, or the long-term costs are less than for the in-house operation.[1]

Types of Microfilm

The type of microfilm stock used will help determine both the clarity and the longevity of the finished product. The film most commonly used for local government records applications is *silver halide* film. This film is essentially the same as that used in conventional black and white photography. Images are obtained by the exposure of visible light on certain silver compounds held in a gelatin emulsion on the surface of the film, and developed through a darkroom process of chemical baths that requires careful control.

Silver halide is the only film that can be certified as "archival" by the American National Standards Institute (ANSI), a nationally recognized agency that establishes standards in this area. "Archival" means that the film stock meets minimum standards prescribed by ANSI and that, when processed, stored, and handled according to ANSI guidelines (cited below), the film will last and maintain its chemical and image stability. Many states require the use of silver halide film, particularly for archival applications or where the original records will be destroyed after filming. Silver halide film has some disadvantages: it has a relatively soft emulsion that is easily scratched, so copies must be made for use. It may deteriorate if stored under high temperatures and/or high humidity. But silver halide film that meets ANSI's archival standards is usually considered as the minimum acceptable for filming records that have long-term or enduring value.[2] Check with the state archival or records management office in your state for information on requirements.

Other types of camera-use film include dry silver and transparent electrophotographic (TEP) film. Dry silver film is developed by a heat process that does not need the wet chemistry required for silver halide film. TEP film, used most often in microfiche applications, can be exposed only a portion at a time, with more images added later to the same film and developed instantaneously. Both may have some advantages over silver halide in terms of speed, flexibility, capacity to be updated, and may be suitable for applications where long-term retention of the information is not a necessity. But neither meets ANSI's archival standards. It is essential to check state requirements before deciding on non-silver halide film for any application.

Two other types of film are available for making *copies* of original, camera-produced film. *Diazo* film uses light-sensitive diazonium salts to produce an image through a process that involves exposure to ultraviolet light and, usually, development through the application of ammonia. Diazo film is very durable, resistant to scratching, and relatively immune to the effects of water and high humidity. Another copy film, *vesicular*, produces an image that consists of small bubbles, or vesicles, by exposing the film to ultraviolet light and then to heat processing. Like diazo, vesicular film is more scratch-resistant than silver film, but it is somewhat susceptible to fading.

Microfilm Formats

There are two basic microfilm formats: *roll film* (primarily reels, cassettes, and cartridges) and *flat film* (film jackets, microfiche, and aperture cards). Reels of film in 16 or 35 mm widths and 100 or 200 foot lengths are most commonly used in records applications. This film is well suited to long series of sequentially organized documents. Roll film can also be purchased in cassettes or cartridges for ease of handling, self-threading, and protection of the film itself. One roll of film can accommodate many images but retrieval of information should be made easier through use of "flash targets" with blank frames to separate groups of related images. These direct the user to the section of the film where the desired image appears, though not to the image itself. Some filming systems number each frame, making it easy for the user to

Fig. 7.2. Microfilm provides information in a compact format that can be retrieved quickly and easily. Its use by local government offices, including law enforcement agencies, makes needed information readily available and can help improve public services. (Montgomery County, Ohio, Microfilming and Records Center)

find any given micro-image. Others use blips or codes that can be read by specially equipped readers and reader-printers. Also available are sophisticated (and expensive) computer-assisted retrieval (CAR) systems that use computers to find desired information. Roll film has a few disadvantages: it is not suited to short series of items, it can be updated only through cutting and splicing the film, and the readers and reader printers that it requires are relatively expensive.

Film jackets are plastic, transparent carriers approximately 4" x 6" in size with channels into which strips of roll film are inserted. Jackets can be given eye-readable titles, can be updated through the insertion of new film, and can be duplicated in the form of microfiche. Microfiche is a sheet of flat film approximately 4" x 6" with micro-images in columns and rows. Eye-readable titles can be added for ease of retrieval. Microfiche is well suited to individual case files that can be copied on a single fiche and to applications where frequent copying and distribution are required.

Aperture cards are cards with a rectangular hole into which a single microimage is mounted and fixed. Aperture cards are widely used for individual maps, engineering drawings, and other large, single-page items. They are eye-readable and can be punched so that they can be sorted or retrieved by machine. Microfiche and aperture cards can also be searched and sorted by computer-assisted retrieval systems.

Which format is best for a given application? The answer depends on a number of factors, including the quantity and nature of the records, how the information will be retrieved and used, need for changes or updating, need for copying and making copies available for use in multiple locations, and relative costs.

Quality Considerations

Exacting quality standards must be maintained to ensure the production of consistently good quality, easily readable, durable microfilm. The state records or archival agency listed in the appendix should be consulted for requirements and guidelines. Two other reliable sources of guidance are the American National Standards Institute (ANSI), 1430 Broadway, New York, NY 10018 and the Association for Information and Image Management (AIIM) (formerly the National Micrographics Association, NMA), 1100 Wayne Avenue, Silver Springs, MD 20910. General suggestions for the production of quality microfilm are as follows:

•*Microfilm stock.* For most applications, the original (camera-produced) film should be fine-gained, high-contrast silver halide microfilm. It should be certified to conform to two ANSI standards: *Specifications for Safety Photographic Film* (ANSI PH 1.25 - 1976, or the latest revision); and *Specifications for Photographic Film for Archival Records, Silver Gelatin Type* (ANSI PH 1.28 - 1981, or the latest revision, for cellulose ester base film; or ANSI PH 1.41 - 1981, or the latest revision, for polyester base films).

•*Completeness.* Filming should be carried out carefully to ensure that all of the records are filmed and that the finished product accurately and faithfully reproduces all of the information.

•*Identification.* The film should be adequately identified and authenticated to indicate what information it contains and to ensure that it can be substituted for the original records in legal and other proceedings. This is done through the preparation of targets with identifying and descriptive information that are filmed along with the records. Identification is spelled out in *Recommended Practice: Identification of Microforms* (ANSI/NMA MS19 - 1978, or latest revision).

•*Readability and reproducibility.* The film should be clear, sharp, and legible, and it should be possible to produce clear paper prints from it. An AIIM publication, *Practices for Operational Procedures/Inspection and Quality Control of First-Generation Silver-Gelatin Microfilm of Documents* (NMA MS23-1981, or the latest revision), covers quality considerations in this area as well as density, resolution, and inspection procedures, which are discussed immediately above.

•*Density.* The film should have a sharp tonal contrast between the information and its background. This contrast is called the "density" of the film and is measured by a device called a densitometer.

•*Resolution.* The images on the film should be sharp and well defined. Microfilm experts use the term "resolution" to describe the sharpness of the film. Resolution is measured by using a microscope to read a special resolution test chart target that is filmed near the beginning of each roll of film.

•*Chemical residue.* Processed film should be tested to ensure that the processing chemicals that could cause image deterioration are thoroughly washed from the film. NMA standard no. MS23-1981, mentioned below, describes the procedures for carrying out these tests. They are also described in more detail in *Methylene Blue Method For Measuring Thiosulfate and Silver Densimetric Method For Measuring Residual Chemicals in Films, Plates, and Papers* (ANSI PH 4.8 - 1978, or latest revision).

•*Inspection.* All film should be thoroughly and completely inspected. NMA publication no. MS 23-1981, cited above, discusses quality controls and inspection procedures.

•*Duplication.* It is advisable to make a duplicate copy of all film to guard against scratching or loss of the original film. Some states require production of a duplicate copy as a condition for approving disposal of the original records.

•*Storage.* Original film should be stored in specially manufactured microfilm containers in secure, clean, surroundings. Temperature and humidity should be controlled with temperatures in the 60-70 degree range and relative humidity around 40 percent. The film should be inspected periodically to ensure that there is no image deterioration. Storage conditions are discussed in *American National Standards Practice for Storage of Processed Safety Photographic Film* (ANSI PH 1.43 - 1979, or latest revision).

Computer Output Microfilm

This chapter has thus far discussed microfilming of paper records. There is, however, another application of microfilm: *COM,* or computer output microfilming. COM systems convert computer-generated data directly from machine-readable form to eye-readable form on microfilm, usually microfiche, with no intermediate paper records being produced. COM has several attractive features: (A) by creating microfilm rather than bulky paper printouts, COM achieves significant cost savings and saves storage space; (B) COM can easily be indexed during the process of production; (C) COM units generate information faster than conventional computer systems which are tied to paper printers; and (D) labor and other production costs, measured in terms of quantity of information produced, are likely to be less than for conventional systems. The main drawback of COM is the expense of the equipment required to produce it. COM is likely to be an economically viable alternative only for large governments that can afford to purchase a COM unit, for governments that can cooperate in the purchase, or for governments that can contract with service agencies with COM capacity.

Notes

1. Michael J. Fox and Kathleen A. McDonough, *Wisconsin Municipal Records Manual* (Madison, 1980), 22-23.

2. For a good summary of archival film, see Howard P. Lowell, "Preservation Microfilming: An Overview," ARMA *Quarterly* XIX (January, 1985), 22-29.

8
Computers and Records Management in Local Government

Technological Change: Challenge and Opportunity

Most local government records are paper-based: familiar, tangible, and fairly easy to manage. Technological changes, however, particularly the introduction of computer technology, are transforming the way information is recorded, manipulated, and stored in local government offices. Some people even predict that computer-based electronic mail and filing will result in paperless offices for local governments. That time is a long way off for most local governments, but computers are becoming increasingly common fixtures. Some local governments own or lease time on large mainframe computers or contract with service agencies that use them. An increasing number of local governments are using smaller personal or microcomputers. These desk top machines are relatively inexpensive, easy to use, and have a storage capacity that only a few years ago would have required much larger machines. Computers are fast, accurate, efficient, and can significantly increase office and agency productivity, a welcome development in an era of increasing local government personnel costs.[1]

Computer technology requires new approaches to information handling. It involves computer disks, tapes, and other "machine-readable" media which fix and maintain information in electronic rather than paper form. Computers give the power to instantly change, update, or eliminate information, literally with the press of a button. The advent of the computer requires us to concentrate on the *information* contained in records as well as the records' physical form. Careful planning is needed to guide the systematic and cost-efficient introduction of computer technology into local government information systems.

Computer Applications in Local Government

Until recently, local government computer applications were limited mainly to financial functions such as calculating and printing bills and paychecks. Today, however, computers are used in a growing variety of housekeeping, management, and information control, and decision-making functions including the following:[2]

• *Office administration.* Computers are used for word processing, files management, indexing of minutes, statistical analyses, strategic planning, and tracking, monitoring, and reporting on office and program performance.

• *Finance.* New, sophisticated spreadsheet programs support complex financial calculations and manipulation that would have been difficult or impossible just a few years ago. Computers are used for accounting, purchasing, accounts receivable and billing, payrolls, and property assessment and tax billing. They are also used for preparation of budgets, monitoring incoming revenues and encumbered expenditures, projecting revenues, and making analyses for decisions on investment or borrowing.

• *Personnel.* Computers are keeping track of recruitment and placement, employee personnel information, and training and development.

• *Public safety.* Police and fire departments are using computers for crime and fire reporting, dispatch, stolen/recovered property, officer activity, patrol scheduling, traffic violation processing, accident reports, court schedules, fire incident analysis, vehicle and equipment maintenance, and other purposes.

• *Public works.* Computers are being used for traffic pattern analysis, vehicle and equipment maintenance, street maintenance and repair planning, work orders, and keeping track of street lights and traffic signals.

• *Licensing and regulation.* Local governments use computers to keep track of licenses issued and renewed and to track other regulatory functions.

• *Community development.* These offices use computers for building permits, inspection scheduling, land use data, and capital expenditure projection.

• *Parks and recreation.* Use here includes park facilities inventories, maintenance, and recreation scheduling.

• *Libraries.* Local libraries are using computers to present on-line catalogs on their holdings, to keep track of inventory, and to keep track of circulation.

•*Records control.* Computers are used to keep track of records in records centers and archives and to locate records in an office, agency, or local government relating to particular topics.

Problems and Challenges with Computers

Computers are still a relatively new phenomenon in local government offices. Local officials often encounter problems in deciding which computers, and which automated systems, best meet their needs. Among the problems are the following:

• Automation is a rapidly developing, constantly changing field. New equipment and software are introduced on practically a daily basis, making comparing and selecting equipment and systems difficult.

• Automation is a highly technical area with its own terminology and vocabulary, which can be confusing. Sales personnel may be of limited assistance to the local official who needs basic information and advice.

• Equipment made by one company often is not compati-

Fig. 8.1 PC's — personal computers — are an increasingly common sight in local government offices. They enable government employees to rapidly create, process, save, and use information, but they also introduce difficult records managment challenges. (American Association for State and Local History)

ble with that made by other companies. Software designed for one brand or model of computer may not work with another. A local government can wind up with equipment that cannot work compatibly or share data.

• Professional records managers and archivists have not yet developed adequate guidelines and standards for dealing with computers and machine-readable records. Helpful assistance and guidance is difficult to find. There is considerable published literature on computers and software, but most of it is highly technical and not geared to local government applications.

• State guidelines and advisory services in this area are limited. Some states can offer advice on physical preservation of machine-readable records but few have information on planning and implementation of automated information systems. It is advisable to check with the state archives or records office listed in Appendix I, however, before planning

an automated system, to secure whatever help and advice is available.
- The potential of computers in information generation and manipulation is still not fully understood. Realizing the potential of computers first requires careful and time-consuming analysis of record keeping needs and practices. Local officials who do not go through this analysis may be disappointed when a computer fails to solve all their records and information problems. A computer is not "... some kind of miracle box which will produce needed information on demand ... not a be-all, end-all solution to every information problem."[3]
- The consequences of a wrong decision can be costly. "The great rush to automate is on ... but it is becoming increasingly clear to local officials that buying a computer is far more complicated than buying a vehicle for the Highway Department and that the penalties for making a wrong decision are far more devastating. The computer can speed things up, but it can also slow down the entire operation" if it is not suited to the local government's needs and requirements.[4]

Determining the Need for a Computer System

Would a microcomputer materially assist your office's work? Should your local government contract with a service agency for large scale computer services? There are no easy answers and the search for solutions requires careful analysis of information needs and available options. Many local governments, particularly smaller ones that do not have systems analysis expertise, may feel the need for outside expert consultation in undertaking the task. In some states, university-based technical assistance programs are available to provide assistance to local governments at no cost or for a nominal fee. Some state archival or records offices can offer advice. Local government associations may also be of assistance. Sometimes, a local government can learn much from its neighbor that has gone through the same process. The process requires a number of steps. They are briefly summarized below.[5]

• *Study the existing records system.* Determine "... where information comes from, who needs it, what is done with it, and what happens because of it."[6] How well do existing records systems work? Would improved records management practices streamline records creation and control and possibly make an automated system unnecessary?

• *Determine information requirements.* What local government computing and management information requirements are not being met through the existing systems? Does the government need a computer to satisfy them? How would they be met through a computer system? What departments would be able to use it? How often would the system be used for inquiry or retrieval? What reports or other products would be produced, how often, and who would use them? How much time would be saved compared to the way things are done now?

• *Explore software and hardware options.* What software is available to perform the function or functions that have been identified? Software (instructions or computer programs which operate the physical equipment of a computer and manipulate data) is the most important part of a computer system because it determines what the system can and will do. What hardware (the physical equipment of a computer system) is available? What local governments have made use of this software and hardware? With what results?

• *Service bureau or in-house?* The decision depends on cost, data processing needs, and volume of work. A service bureau can offer trained personnel with reliable experience, economy for bulk operations, overload capacity, and assistance with systems development if needed. In-house development requires purchasing or leasing equipment, purchasing or developing appropriate software, training current workers or hiring new ones, and assuming continuing responsibility for maintenance of the computer system. It has some advantages, however: the system can give custom, on-demand, responsive service, it can be modified as new needs arise, and it may be less expensive in the long run than an outside service bureau.

- *Calculate costs.* A cost-benefit analysis is needed to weigh probable benefits against probable costs. Costs include both fixed costs, such as purchase of computer equipment and supplies, and variable costs such as expanded purchase or lease of additional computer equipment to meet future needs. Benefits are both tangible (reduction in redundant paperwork, reduction in time spent looking through paper files for information, greater efficiency in production of studies, reports, etc.) and intangible (easier availability of information needed to carry on work, ability to draw on and use all the information sources that pertain to an issue or problem, improvement in quality of administration, etc.).

Once the decision is made, there will need to be a period of testing to provide employees with an opportunity to get used to the new system and for checking to ensure that it meets all the local government's requirements. During the time of testing, it is advisable to retain the records system that the new computer system is replacing or superseding. After that, with complete reliance on the new system, ongoing monitoring and evaluation are recommended to check the responsiveness of the new system and the need, if any, for modifications and requirements.

All computer systems should be "documented" through writing down, or retaining, information describing the development, characteristics, and capacity of the system. This includes analytical documentation created or collected during the study phase that describes system requirements; development documentation, describing the system in detail; and operational documentation on how it operates. Documentation helps instruct users in the system and provides an understanding of how to modify, refine, or expand the system.

Care and Preservation of Machine-Readable Records

Computer tapes and disks, used to record and store data in computer systems, are not regarded as long-term storage media. There are no generally recognized industry standards that indicate their durability or probable lifespan. One expert estimates that computer tapes, the most common storage devices for large amounts of data, when stored under optimal conditions, can be expected to last no more than from twelve to twenty years.[7] Until a new and better electronic storage medium becomes available, material with long-term value should either be printed onto paper, produced as computer output microfilm (COM), or transferred periodically to new tape. It is also advisable to make a duplicate, or backup copy, of such records whenever possible.

Computer tapes should be stored under secure conditions with carefully controlled temperatures (in the 60 - 70 degree range) and relative humidity (35 - 45 percent range). Fluctuations in either temperature or humidity should be avoided. The storage area should be free from dust, dirt, and strong magnetic fields. The tapes should be inspected, cleaned, and rewound periodically. Once every few years, samples should be tested to identify signal deterioration or errors. If evidence of deterioration appears that cannot be corrected by cleaning and rewinding the tape, the information should be transferred to a new tape.[8]

Scheduling Machine-Readable Records

Computers record information in the form of magnetic or electronic impulses on tapes, disks, or other computer system storage devices. Unless the system is used simply to create a paper-based or microfilm-based records, by most definitions the information on the tape or disk is to be considered an official record. The information on the tape or disk is referred to as being in "machine-readable" form, meaning it can only be processed directly by a computer. Machine-readable records should be treated the same as other records and scheduled after analysis of their administrative, fiscal, legal, and other values. This is a highly complex area where little guidance is available at the present time.

The appraisal checklist at the end of this chapter indicates some of the intellectual and technical considerations that need to be taken into account when appraising and setting retention periods for machine-readable records. The process needs to be carried out early in the life of a computer system. Files that are used for processing or to create, correct, revise, or derive output from master files should probably be assigned a short retention period that amounts to permission to erase and reuse on a convenience basis. Master data files are of greater importance and warrant longer retention periods. Other appraisal factors, particularly important when deciding which records have archival value, include the following:[9]

- *Level of aggregation.* Generally, "micro-level" (detailed) data is desirable to allow future aggregation, manipulation, and analysis. Consequently, machine-readable records that have detailed data are more likely to be of value than those with summary information.

- *Format.* If the information exists in both machine-readable form and in hard copy form (for instance, as input or output documents), it is important to anticipate how the information is likely to be retrieved and used before deciding how long to keep the machine-readable form.

- *Updates.* In many systems, the information is updated each day or on some other periodic basis. The content of the records therefore changes constantly. If the system preserves only current information, then that is all that can be captured and saved at any given time. If, on the other hand, the system retains a record of all transactions, then it may be possible to retain information for an extended period. This is an important consideration in scheduling the records.

- *Access restrictions.* Machine-readable records may hold information that is closed or restricted under Freedom of Information, personal privacy, or other statutes. This may affect appraisal and schedulings decisions.
- *Readability.* The machine-readable records must be in good enough physical shape to be readable and usable.
- *Software dependence.* If machine-readable records require particular software in order to be used and read, then that software must be preserved and available or else the information must be transferred to a format that does not require special software.
- *Hardware dependence.* Some machine-readable files require specific computer equipment. If this equipment is unavailable or is obsolete, the information must be reformatted so that it can be read and used with available equipment.
- *Costs.* Costs include the cost of the tape or other machine-readable format for data storage and the cost of a duplicate or back-up file. Magnetic tape is a very compact storage medium, and storage costs, when compared to paper records for comparable quantities of data, are economical. Costs can rise rapidly, however, if staff time and technical assistance are needed to reformat the data, to search for, correct, or reconstruct documentation, or to salvage deteriorated or damaged media.

Notes

1. James R. Griesemer, *Microcomputers in Local Government* (Washington, 1982), 18-22.

2. *Ibid.,* 26; "Microsoftware News," bimonthly newsletter issued by International City Management Association, issues from January 1984 onward.

3. Jack Hawley-Widmar, "Designing an Information System," *Information and Records Management,* 17 (June 1982), 37.

4. Robert Vitello, "Computerizing Local Government: Caveat Emptor," *Empire State Report,* (November 1983), 29.

5. See Donald F. Norris, *Microcomputers and Local Government: A Hand-*

book (Omaha, 1984), 24-35, for a very clear account of how local governments should analyze needs for microcomputers.

6. National Center for State Courts, *Automated Information Systems: Planning and Implementation* (n.p., 1983), 3.

7. Margaret L. Hedstrom, *Archives and Manuscripts: Machine-Readable Records* (Chicago, 1984), 15.

8. See Sidney B. Geller, *Care and Handling of Computer Magnetic Storage Media,* issued by the National Bureau of Standards (Washington, 1983).

9. Hedstrom, *Machine-Readable Records,* 41 - 45. See also Charles Dollar, "Appraising Machine-Readable Records," *American Archivist,* 61 (October 1978), 423-430.

Appraisal Checklist for Machine-Readable Records

This checklist indicates some of the factors to be considered in the appraisal of machine-readable records. From State Historical Society of Wisconsin, *Procedures Manual for Machine-Readable Records* (Madison, 1983), 3.

Intellectual Considerations:

Does the data file have:			
legal value?	Yes ☐	No ☐	Maybe ☐
evidential value?	Yes ☐	No ☐	Maybe ☐
informational value?	Yes ☐	No ☐	Maybe ☐
Does the data file have:			
immediate research value?	Yes ☐	No ☐	Maybe ☐
long-term research value?	Yes ☐	No ☐	Maybe ☐
Does the data file contain original micro-level data?	Yes ☐	No ☐	
Is the file likely to be used for:			
statistical analysis?	Yes ☐	No ☐	Maybe ☐
retrieval of single cases?	Yes ☐	No ☐	Maybe ☐

Is the data file?   One time study? ☐   Ongoing? ☐

Is the data file:
  In danger of deterioration
  or destruction in its present
  location?   Yes ☐   No ☐   Maybe ☐

Do similar records exist
elsewhere?   Yes ☐   No ☐
  Are they: Hardcopy ☐   Microforms ☐
  Covered by an RDA   Yes ☐   No ☐
  (Records Disposition
  Authorization)?   RDA# _____

Do related records contain
information not included in
the data file?   Yes ☐   No ☐

Does the data file contain
information not included in
related records?   Yes ☐   No ☐

Are related records more
desirable
  re: the cost of
  preservation?   Yes ☐   No ☐
  re: arrangement?   Yes ☐   No ☐

Will the other records be
preserved?   Yes ☐   No ☐

Are there restrictions on use:
  of textual records?   Yes ☐   No ☐
  of machine-readable
  records?   Yes ☐   No ☐

Technical Considerations:

Is the data file readable?   Yes ☐   No ☐
Is the documentation complete?   Yes ☐   No ☐
Is special software required?   Yes ☐   No ☐
Approximate volue of hard copy records: _____
Approximate number of logical records: _____
Logical records length: _____

9
Management of Archival Records

Archival Records: A Local Government Asset

Archives are records worthy of permanent preservation because of the importance of their information for continuing administrative, legal, or fiscal purposes, or for historical or other research. There is no definitive way to identify all of a local government's archival records but the appraisal process, described in Chapter IV, should succeed in identifying most of them. Archives comprise only a small percentage of all the records but their importance to government and to researchers is immense. They are, or ought to be, among every community's most prized possessions. Most local governments, however, do not give their archival records adequate care and preservation. Why not? Some misconceptions about archives and archival programs may stand in the way:

• *"Archives are dusty old records from the remote past."* Actually, they are vital information resources and include records created yesterday as well as those from the community's earliest days.

• *"Only antiquarians with narrow historical interests really care about and use archives."* Not so! Local government itself may be the main user of its own archival records. They also support a variety of historical and other research of importance to the public at large.

• *"We don't need an archival program."* **Every** local government needs to provide for the care of its archival records. They are too important an investment — in terms of governmental resources that produced them and their value to government, to citizens, and to historians — not to preserve them.

• *"We can't afford an archival program."* In a sense, local government can't afford *not* to have one. Moreover, the fundamentals of archival programming are not expensive and there is a return in terms of information being available when needed.

• *"Archives are fine but have nothing to do with records management."* Actually, an archival program is part of a total records management effort. Attention to archival records includes scheduling, preservation, and, for most, passing them through an inactive phase before they get to the local government's archival facility.

• *"We'd like to do something with our archives but don't know where to begin."* It's not mysterious or terribly difficult. Every local government can establish at least the basics of an archival program. This chapter provides an overview and additional advice is available through several of the readings listed in Chapter X, from state archival agencies, and from other sources.

Archives: Contribution to Government

An archival program benefits local government. "Archives exist to serve the parent body, and other uses, while salutary, are still secondary ... Archives have a definite, beneficial function, rooted in day-to-day practicality. Each time a department head can check an annual report, a worker can verify a disability or a pension claim, or past trends or performances be evaluated in planning for the future, the archives is validated."[1] Archival records support the government in at least three ways:

• *They include the operational foundation documents of government.* Archival records such as minutes, resolutions, local laws, and ordinances are the legal bases for the government's very existence. They underlie and give authority to its operations. They are constantly referenced, studied, cited, and used as a basis for policy development and the delivery of services. Even the older ones may have currency for ongoing governmental operations.

- *They provide legal documentation and protection.* Certain records are essential for protecting the government and defining its legal rights and responsibilities. These include deeds to government-owned property; legally binding agreements, some of which have implications long after their expiration; and maps that show the right of way of public streets and highways and the official boundaries of geopolitical subdivisions. They also include reports and studies that had an important impact on or changed the direction of local governmental policy.

- *They help local officials learn from the past and ensure policy continuity.* "Our archival records provide details about past decisions and actions," says a brochure from one city archives. "This information is needed by administrators when they make similar decisions now and in the future."[2] These records with information on organization, functions, activities, and methods of procedure "are indispensable to the government itself ... they are a storehouse of administrative wisdom and experience ... They contain precedents for policies, procedures, and the like, and can be used as a guide for public administrators in solving problems of the present that are similar to others dealt with in the past."[3] Local government officers can — and do — use these materials to study the origins of policies, to analyze program development, and to construct policy that flows from and is consistent with the past.

Archives: Protection of Legal Rights

"People and organizations require historical records to support legal claims. Contracts, taxation records, maps, and legislative materials are some of the many items useful for this purpose."[4] Local governments in many states are responsible for recording births, deaths, and marriages, vital to individuals' rights. Deeds, other property records, and wills and estate records, show ownership and transfer of title to property. These fundamental legal documents protect citizens' rights to inherit and possess property. Original maps show legal boundaries between parcels of land, essential in determining property lines and in settling disputes. School and other educational records document educational attainments. Court records show the results of issues and controversies that were settled through legal processes. Local attorneys, including those working for local governments, frequently use local government archival records to substantiate legal claims.

Fig. 9.1 Local government archival records are invaluable research resources for the government itself and for local and state history. The records must be arranged, described, preserved, and made available in order to ensure their survival and promote their use. (Metropolitan Nashville-Davidson County Archives, Tennessee)

Archives: Research into Contemporary Problems and Issues

Archival records can provide information for meeting practical, everyday issues and problems. For example, public interest groups may delve into archival records to study the origin and development of problems and issues. Community planners use archival records to trace the historical development of particular areas in the community. Builders, engineers, and surveyors — from both government and the private sector — use archives for research into the infrastructure. They consult maps, plans, sketches, and specifications on the location, age, and construction of bridges, highways, sewer and water lines, etc. Home owners, engineers, architects, and historic preservationists use building department plans, files, and reports in their work to restore and preserve historically significant structures. These records help determine the original appearance and alert builders to hidden structural components. Such records may also be important for concerns directly relating to public welfare, such as locating toxic waste dumps, tracing the flow of underground streams, and as background information for a variety of ecological issues.[5]

Archives: Historical Research

Local government archival records are rich historical research resources. They contain information on the development of the communities the government served and on the people whom government served, regulated, taxed, incarcerated, and otherwise came into contact with. These records are used for at least four types of historical research:

• *History of the government.* Archival records that document the origin, development, functions, activities, and methods of government are rich sources for studies in governmental history. In fact, they may be the only available sources for analyzing many of the government's approaches to dealing with organizational, procedural, and policy matters.[6]

- *Community history.* Since government is a central community institution, many important aspects of a community's history are likely to be reflected in its local government records. The records "reveal a great deal about individuals, groups, and conditions within the community, the evolution of issues and public policies, the characteristics and uses of buildings and property, the development of transportation systems, and other local phenomena."[7] Local government archival records are used by local historians and by historical scholars making comparative studies of communities. They are also increasingly used in school social studies and history classes to make community history come alive for students.

- *Social history.* Researchers interested in social history make use of poll books, census records, welfare records, tax rolls, real estate and inheritance records, and other material, to reconstruct past social conditions. Often, the detailed information in the records can be used in the aggregate for broad generalizations over time. Increasing imaginative use of computers by historians opens up even more possibilities for summarizing and manipulating the information, for combining information from two or more records series, and for analyzing changes over time.

- *Genealogical and family history.* "You may not know much about government, but your government has always known a lot about you and your ancestors," says a manual on local history research. "All the highlights and turns of fortune in life have long been recorded somewhere in the official records: birth, death, taxes, inheritances, licenses, marriage and divorce, property transfers, bankruptcies, and lawsuits."[8] Such records are important resources for tracing individual's lives, family life, marriage patterns, and intergroup relations. They also help historians reconstruct the political, economic, and social context in which individuals and families lived and acted.

Archival Records: Whose Responsibility?

Local governments are the creators of archival records, need them for government business, and have an obligation — to the people and posterity — to preserve them for historical and other research. There are at least three different approaches for a local government to meet this responsibility.

The first, and the best in most cases, is for the government to establish and maintain its own archival program. This is, in fact, virtually the *only* option open in states whose laws prohibit transfer of archival records out of local officials' custody. It clearly fixes responsibility where it belongs, with the local government that owns the records. It keeps the archives near at hand, secure, and easily accessible when needed by local officials and others. A variation on this approach is for two or more local governments to cooperate on a joint archival programming effort, where state law permits. This cooperative approach permits sharing of facilities and resources but keeps responsibility and control in the hand of local officials.

Some local governments transfer their archival records to local institutions such as libraries and historical societies. This places the records alongside other community historical materials in settings with concerned professionals to watch over them, but there are several drawbacks. The archival records lose some of their character as an organic part of government and are treated like ordinary historical materials. The custody and responsibility for the records may become unclear and access questions become complicated. The receiving institution may regard the government materials as archival stepchildren that do not warrant as much care and attention as its other holdings. Over the years, interest may wane and resources diminish until the local government archival materials cease to receive adequate care. As noted above, state law may prevent such a transfer and, even if it is permissible, the approval of the state archival agency should be secured beforehand. If this option is taken, the local government and the receiving repository should draw up a detailed transfer or deposit agreement. It should spell out who has continuing responsibility for care, protection, arrangement, description, reference services, and other functions.

A number of states permit and encourage a third option for local government archival records: transfer to state-approved or state-sponsored regional centers or to the state archives. This approach ensures that the records are housed in secure facilities and unites them with other local government records from the region or the state. The centralized approach lays the basis for systematic documentation of the governmental history of a region or the state. It measurably assists researchers with topics that require looking at the records of several local governments. There are also some disadvantages: local governments lose direct control and the records are located at a distance from their home communities and therefore not immediately available when needed.

An Archival Program: a Continuing Endeavor

A local government archival *program* administered and supported by the local government itself is much more than just a one-time effort to preserve the oldest or most valuable records. The program should be seen as dynamic; it will continue to grow as long as government functions and produces archival records. The need to provide for continuity has a number of implications:

• *Authority.* The archival program's authority, responsibilities, and goals should be spelled out in the local government's records ordinance or elsewhere.

• *Responsibility.* The archival program should be developed as part of, or in close conjunction with, other records management efforts. One person — the records management officer or someone who will work for or closely with him or her — should be assigned coordinating responsibility.

- *Growth.* An archival program should be expected to grow. The inventory, appraisal, and records retention and disposition procedures described in Chapters III and IV, will identify series of archival records. Most of these should come to the archival facility for permanent preservation after a specified number of years in originating offices and, possibly, in inactive storage. The only exceptions are likely to be records such as deed books that are "archival" but that nonetheless need to be retained for use in their offices of origin.
- *Custody.* The records ordinance or some other document should establish clearly who has both physical and legal custody of archival records that are formally transferred to the archival facility.
- *Resources.* The legislative body and chief administrative officer must make sure that the archival program has enough resources to take care of the archival records in an acceptable manner on a continuing basis.
- *Facilities.* Archival records should be stored in a clean, secure, fireproof environment. There must be enough storage capacity to accommodate the archival records that are expected to be received over several years. A separate room or even a separate building may be needed, depending on the quantity of the archival records. The inactive records center, described in Chapter VI, may serve as the archival storage center provided it meets security and other requirements and that one area can be designated for archival records.

Preservation of Archival Records

Every archival program has an obligation to preserve the material under its charge. Preservation includes several factors, the first being physical security. Archives should be kept in a secure facility accessible only to the people responsible for them, to prevent theft of misplacement. There should be oversight of researchers to guard against mishandling and theft. The storage facility should have steel shelving and the records should be placed in acid-free file folders and records cartons to help prolong their longevity. Clean air and good circulation are important; air conditioning is highly desirable. Temperature and humidity must be closely controlled; temperatures should be in the 65 to 75 degree range, and relative humidity in the 30 to 60 percent range, with special provisions as needed for microfilm, computer tapes, and other non-paper records.

The person or people responsible for the archives should be able to provide basic cleaning and, if they have appropriate training, may provide other basic conservation measures. More serious preservation problems should be referred to a professional conservator. One other approach to consider is duplication of key archival records, by microfilming or other means. This approach provides a security copy of the records, reduces unnecessary handling of the originals by making the copies available, and makes it easy to disseminate the information wherever it is needed.[9]

Arrangement and Description

When they arrive at the archival facility, records may need to be weeded of extraneous, duplicate, and non-record material. They should be placed in acid-free files and cartons. The records should be systematically arranged to facilitate use. Two basic principles govern arrangement. The first is that records from different offices or origin or from different sources should be kept separate and should not be intermingled. The second is that, whenever possible, records should be retained in their original organizational pattern and original filing arrangement so that they may be studied sequentially in the same order in which they were created and filed. If this original order has been lost, records should be arranged or grouped in a logical order to facilitate their use.

The records should be systematically described so that they can and will be used. The archival program should develop

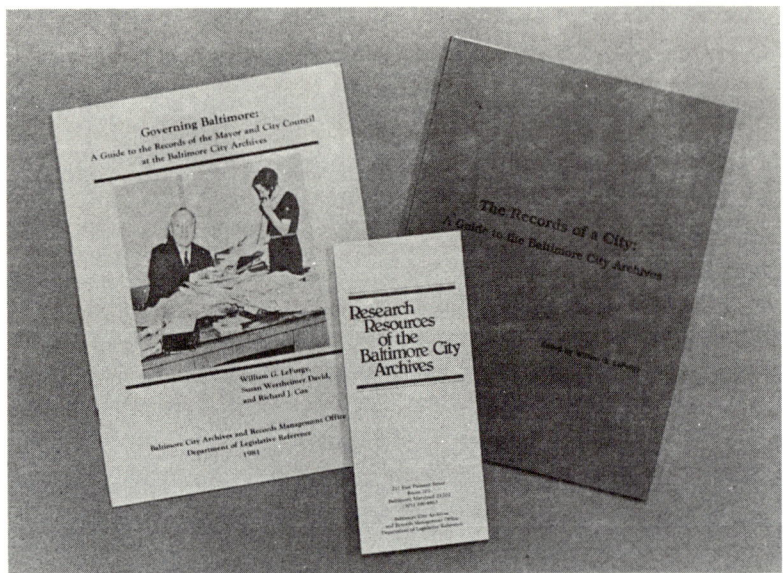

Fig. 9.2. Lists of archival records and other finding aids can be developed to help encourage the use of archival records by both government officials and outside researchers. Increased use will, in turn, bring attention and support to the archival program. (Baltimore City Archives and Records Management Office)

a system of descriptive "finding aids" that enable the people in charge of the archives to retrieve materials and that provide essential information about them for users. Finding aids should concentrate first on large groups of records and then series before attempting to describe individual items. A brief description of all records is preferable to a very detailed description of only a small percentage of them. It may be helpful to include descriptions of archival records that will stay in their offices of origin and not be transferred to the archives, as well as those that are in the archives. The level of description depends on the records' research value, their physical condition, the anticipated level of demand, how users are likely to want to retrieve information, and on the practical matter of how much time is available to prepare the finding aids. Finding aids may include, as appropriate, guides, inventories, special lists, shelf and box lists, indexes, and for machine-readable records, documentation of software.[10]

Many local governments have found it possible to cooperate with historical societies or to use volunteers in arrangement and description of archival records. This strategy may work well if the records management officer or person in charge of the archives first provides basic orientation and training and also closely supervises the work.

Reference Services and Promotional Activities

Archival records are saved and managed *only* for the purpose of being *used*. The archival program must provide opportunities and encouragement for use of the records it holds. The archival facility should be open for research use on a regular and stated schedule if possible. It should provide adequate space and facilities for government officials and others who wish to use the records. The records should be open to use by any responsible researcher with restrictions in line with state and/or local privacy and access laws and regulations. The person in charge of the archival material should be present when the archives is open to assist researchers, retrieve materials, and answer questions.[11]

Archival programs need to be *promoted* by the people who administer them, for a number of reasons. First, local government officials themselves need to be reminded of the value of archival records and the importance of the archival program. Second, citizens need to understand the importance of the archives and of the programs that preserve them. Third, the research potential of local government archival records is largely unrecognized by government officials, historical and other researchers, and other citizens. Without special efforts to draw attention to these materials, utilization of them may be disappointingly low.

A local government archival program should reach out — to government officials, to historians, and to other citizens — to explain the importance of the archival program and to promote the maximum use of the archival records by anyone who can make beneficial use of them. Descriptive guides to the archives are very helpful in this regard and can be supplemented by special lists of records with particular interest. Workshops and training programs for local officials, historians, and others, can help expose the research potential of the records. Lectures, exhibits, and other public programs aimed at researchers and the general public are useful ways of getting the promotional message across. Working with groups with special interests in the materials can also be helpful. For instance, it may be possible to interest local schools in using copies of selected archival records in social studies and community history courses.[12]

Notes

1. Robert W. Arnold, III, "Why Should We Even Have An Archives?," in New York State Archives, *Managing Local Government Records* (Albany, 1985), 67-69.

2. "Research Resources of the Baltimore City Archives," (Brochure, Baltimore, n.d.).

3. Theodore R. Schellenberg, *Modern Archives: Principles and Techniques* (Chicago, 1956), 140.

4. "Research Resources of the Baltimore City Archives."

5. "Archives: What They Are, Why They Matter," Society of American Archivists *Newsletter,* (May 1984), 6.

6. Schellenberg, *Modern Archives,* 140.

7. David E. Kyvig and Myron A. Marty, *Nearby History: Exploring the World Around You* (Nashville, 1982), 91.

8. Thomas E. Felt, *Researching, Writing, and Publishing Local History* (Nashville, 1976), 43.

9. Two good starting points for more information on preservation are: George M Cunha, "Conserving Local Archival Materials on a

Limited Budget," *American Association for State and Local History Technical Leaflet* no. 86 (November, 1975), and Mary Lynn Ritzenthaler, *Archives and Manuscripts: Conservation* (Chicago, 1983).

10. The Society of American Archivists' *Evaluation of Archival Institutions: Services, Principles, and Guide to Self-Study* (Chicago, 1982), 20-22, succinctly outlines the essential elements of an archival program. David B. Gracy, II, *Archives and Manuscripts: Arrangement and Description* (Chicago, 1977), one of the Society's "Basic Manuals," introduces the topics of arrangement and description.

11. Sue E. Holbert, *Archives and Manuscripts: Reference and Access* (Chicago, 1977).

12. Ann E. Pederson and Gail Farr Casterline, *Archives and Manuscripts: Public Programs* (Chicago, 1982).

Local Government Records: Importance for Local History

Many local government records are invaluable for research into local and community history. From H.G. Jones, *Local Government Records: An Introduction to Their Management, Preservation, and Use* (Nashville, 1980), 107-108.

...since the modern bureaucracy simply cannot function without records, it is safe to assume that nearly all units of [local] government — counties, cities, towns, villages, boroughs, parishes, court districts, school districts, fire districts, public utility districts, drainage districts, and other special purpose districts — create records that tell something about or affect the lives of the people that they serve. The records were created in connection with the day-to-day functions of public offices, but many of them   particularly those of older counties and towns — have value for purposes for which they were never intended. They offer grist for the historian's mill. And what grist it is! Records of births, deaths, marriages, property ownership, settlement of estates, taxes, voting; records of ordinances and regulations, of complaints and charges, of crime and punishment, of trials and verdicts, of the insane and the destitute, of fires and floods, of plagues and quarantines, of behavior and curfew, of taverns and bakeries, of slaves and masters, of wives and husbands, of fences and roads, of earthquakes and wars. Records of local government constitute America's cupboard of unspoiled goodies, often peeked at or smelled by the curious, occasionally fondled and nibbled by amateur historians and genealogists, sometimes prepared and served up on a delectable platter by scholars. A smorgasbord of manuscripts, the richness of which is concealed by their classification as simply 'old records.'

10
Where to Turn for More Help

This chapter briefly discusses several resources to which local officials can turn for more help with their records problems.

Other Local Governments

Some of the most pressing records management problems are common to many local government offices all over the nation. Solutions developed and applied in one jurisdiction may be useful in others. Therefore, local governments in a region, within a state, or even on an interstate basis should systematically communicate to learn from each other. Possible approaches include: (1) articles on model programs in newsletters of state associations of local government officials; (2) sessions devoted to records at meetings of these associations; (3) records workshops organized by these associations or by local officials within a region; (4) exchange of local records ordinances, procedures manuals, handbooks, and guides to archival records; and (5) visits to other local governments to see how they have solved records problems. Some local governments may wish to take one additional step and develop cooperative approaches to common problems and needs, e.g. cooperative storage, microfilming, automated data processing, and other services.

State Archival and Records Management Agencies

The state offices listed in Appendix I can provide advice on records retention and disposition, microfilming, and other aspects or records management. Some of these agencies issue publications, hold workshops, and have records specialists available to consult with individual local governments on records management problems.

Associations of Local Government Officials

Most states have associations of town, county, city, or other local government officials. These associations, through newsletters and other publications, workshops, and annual meetings, can serve as means for exchange of information on local government records matters, as noted above. They can also serve their members by working for improved records legislation and state advisory services. Several national associations of local government officials may also be helpful in facilitating exchange of information and providing workshops, publications, and other materials that may assist with records problems. Among these associations are:

International Association of Clerks, Recorders, Election Officials, and Treasurers (IACREOT), P.O. Box 790, Vidalia, LA 71373.
> Includes officials of cities, counties, and other governments. Publishes a quarterly newspaper and holds annual meetings with some records-related sessions and workshops on local government problems.

International City Management Association (ICMA), 1120 G Street, Suite 300, Washington, DC 20005.
> A professional organization of appointed chief management executives in local government. Issues a monthly magazine, a bi-weekly newsletter, a bi-monthly newsletter on microcomputers in local government, and books and

other publications on management, and a management information service on a subscription basis.

International Institute of Municipal Clerks (IIMC), 160 N. Altadena Drive, Pasadena, CA 91107.

Includes city, village, town, and county clerks. Issues a monthly newsletter, news releases, announcements, and publications, including a series of "Technical Bulletins," some of which cover indexing of minutes, record disposition, filing systems, and other aspects of records management. Includes a standing committee on records management. Holds an annual meeting and sponsors education and professional certification programs.

National Association of Counties (NACO) and its affiliates, including **National Association of County Recorders and Clerks (NACRC)**, 440 First Street, N.W., Washington, DC 20001.

Includes county officials. Issues a newsletter, carries out research, holds workshops, and serves as an information clearinghouse. NACO's annual meeting sometimes features records-related sessions organized by NACRC.

National Association of Towns and Townships, 1522 K Street, N.W. suite 730, Washington, DC 20005.

Provides technical assistance, educational services, and public policy support to local government officials of small communities. Publishes monthly reports and policy seminar reports. Holds an annual meeting each fall.

National League of Cities, 1301 Pennsylvania Avenue, N.W., Washington, DC 20004.

Includes individual cities and state municipal leagues as members. Publishes a weekly abstract of articles on urban affairs and a weekly newsletter on federal, state, and local developments of interest to cities. Also issues publications on city finances and other aspects of urban government management.

National Associations of Records and Information Professionals

A number of national associations specialize in records and information management, issue publications, and hold workshops and meetings that may be of interest to local government records administrators. Among them are:

Association for Information and Image Management (AIIM), formerly the National Micrographics Association (NMA), 8719 Colesville Road, Silver Spring, MD 20910.

AIIM, an outgrowth of the National Micrographics Association, "represents the various imaging media in the storage, transfer, and retrieval of information." It publishes a monthly *Journal of Information and Image Management,* issues and updates standards that are widely recognized as authoritative in the micrographics industry, and publishes books and technical manuals on micrographics and information management. AIIM has a number of regional chapters and holds an annual conference which includes an exposition of new micrographics and other information-handling equipment.

Association of Records Managers and Administrators (ARMA), 4200 Somerset Drive, Suite 213, Prairie Village, KS 66208.

ARMA is an association devoted to all aspects of records administration. It promotes research in records management and provides a forum for the exchange of information on records management techniques and developments. It publishes a journal, *Records Management Quarterly,* a monthly newsletter, and technical publications on records management. It has a number of local chapters and an "Industry Action Committee" (IAC) that is concerned with county and municipal records. It holds an annual meeting and sponsors records management training.

National Association of Government Archives and Records Administrators (NAGARA), Executive Secretariat, New York State Archives, 10A75 Cultural Education Center, Albany, NY 12230.

NAGARA is a national association dedicated to improving the management of government records and archives at all levels. It publishes a quarterly newsletter, the *Clearinghouse*, which includes news and feature articles on federal, state and local government records programs. It issues technical publications and carries out special studies and projects. NAGARA also holds an annual meeting with sessions on local government records issues and problems.

National Center for State Courts, 300 Newport Avenue, Williamsburg, VA 23185.

The Center is a nonprofit organization dedicated to modernizing court operations at the state and local levels throughout the nation. It provides education and training for court personnel, conducts research, and serves as a clearinghouse of information. Its publications include manuals on court case management systems, automation, and micrographics systems and standards.

National Information Center for Local Government Records (NICLOG), American Association for State and Local History, 172 Second Avenue North, Suite 102, Nashville, TN 37201.

NICLOG, the publisher of this manual, is a consortium of associations interested in improving local government records management and preserving historically valuable local government records. It is governed by a policy board that includes representatives of several local government associations and archival and records management groups. NICLOG has available an introductory audiovisual program on local government records management and an introductory brochure, and it administers an information clearinghouse.

Society of American Archivists (SAA), 600 South Federal Street, Suite 504, Chicago, IL 60605.

SAA is the nation's largest association of institutions and individuals interested in archival records. It has an extensive publications program which includes a quarterly journal, the *American Archivist*, a bi-monthly newsletter, a basic manual series, and other publications. SAA holds a national meeting each year and sponsors workshops on archival techniques. It also has "Sections" for members with similar interests, including one on government records.

Some local government records and information specialists may be interested in professional associations with more specialized interests. There are several associations whose interests are primarily in the area of automation, information exchange, telecommunications, and other advances in information and communications technology. Among them are:

American Society for Information Science (ASIS), 1010 16th Street, N.W., Washington, DC 20036.

Includes information specialists, scientists, librarians, administrators, and others interested in the "use, organization, storage, retrieval, evaluation, and dissemination" of recorded information. ASIS publishes a bulletin, journal, and newsletter and holds an annual meeting with sessions devoted to information management.

Associated Information Managers (AIM), 1776 E. Jefferson Street, Suite 470 S, Rockville, MD 20852.

A professional association "dedicated to the integration of information technologies and content" and interested in "all aspects of managing and integrating information." AIM publishes a newsletter and holds an annual meeting with sessions on information sources and systems.

Association of Information Systems Professionals (AISP), 1015 N. York Road, Willow Grove, PA 10990.

AISP's purpose is to "develop and disseminate ideas, methods, and techniques pertaining to the processing of information in the office environment" and to serve those who "design, implement, manage, and use various types of information systems." It publishes a bi-monthly journal and a bi-monthly product newsletter and holds an annual meeting devoted primarily to office automation and information systems.

Publications

There are many publications that will assist local government records administrators, and new ones are being issued continually. This section discusses some of the more useful ones.

State-issued local government records manuals

Several state archival or records agencies have issued manauals for local government in their states. Usually these publications include information on legal records retention and disposition requirements and/or state-issued records retention and disposition schedules and advice on records management. Several of these manuals are listed below; for more information, contact the issuing agency, listed in Appendix I.

Jim Edgar, *Illinois Local Records Management Handbook* (Springfield, 1984); Nancy Mossman, *Iowa Municipal Records Manual* (Des Moines, 1982); Larry Fortson, compiler, Lewis Bellardo, ed., *Commonwealth of Kentucky Local Records Management Manual* (Frankfort, 1981); Division of Archives, Office of the Massachusetts Secretary of State, *Municipal Records Management Manual* (Boston, 1983); New York State Archives, *Managing Local Government Records* (Albany, 1985); Nevada State Library, Division of Archives and Records, *Nevada Local Government*

Records Manual (Carson City, 1983); David Levine, ed., (Ohio) *Local Government Records Handbook* (Columbus, 1984); Local Records Department, Archives Division, Texas State Library, Texas County Records Manual (Austin, 1978); State of Washington, Department of General Administration, *Local Government Records Workshop Handbook* (Olympia, n.d.); and Michael J. Fox and Kathleen A. McDonough, *Wisconsin Municipal Records Manual* (Madison, 1980). In addition, some of the states have issued manuals on conservation, micrographics, and other elements of records management.

Federal government publications

The National Archives and Records Administration (NARA), formerly the National Archives and Records Service (NARS) issued a series of *Records Management Handbooks* from 1960 to 1974, covering forms analysis, filing, information retrieval, microfilming, and automation. Many of these handbooks are still useful. More recently, the National Archives has published new manuals in the same series, including *Federal Archives and Records Centers* (Washington, 1979), *File Stations* (1980), *Subject Filing* (1981), *File Equipment and Supplies* (1981), *Disposition of Federal Records* (1981), and *Case Filing* (1983). The Archives is also issuing handbooks in a series of "Self-Inspection Guides for Federal agencies," including *Evaluating a Vital Records Program* (1983), and *Evaluating Files Maintenance and Records Disposition Programs* (1984). These publications are issued for federal agencies but most include information useful to local governments. For information on the availability of these and other National Archives' publications, contact National Archives and Records Administration, National Archives Building, Washington, DC 20408.

Another federal agency, the Office of Information Resources Management, General Services Administration, has also issued handbooks that may be useful to local governments. These include *End Users Guide to Buying Small Computers* (Washington, 1984), and a series of "Self Inspection Guides for Agencies," including *Evaluating Copy Management* (1984), *Evaluating Micrographics Management* (1984), and *Evaluating End Use Computing* (1984). For information on the availability of these and other publications of this office, contact Office of Information Resources Management, General Services Administration, Washington, DC 20405.

Publications of professional associations

Several of the professional associations noted above have issued publications that contain information useful to local government records administrators. The *Association of Records Managers and Administrators* (ARMA) has published a series of "Technical Reports," including Giovanna B. Seguin and Carrie Miller Townley, *Introduction to Filing Systems* (1981), Phyllis M. Lybarger, *Records Retention Scheduling* (1980), Marjorie E. Carson, *Records Supervisors' Responsibilities* (1980), and Douglas M. Haire, *An Organizational Concept for Information Management Programs* (1980). ARMA has also issued a *Bibliography on Records Management* by Patricia A. Michaels (1980), a series of slides on records management for use with an accompanying *Records Management Workshop* manual (n.d.), and several other publications.

The *Society of American Archivists* (SAA) has published Frank B. Evans, comp., *Modern Archives and Manuscripts: A Select Bibliography* (Chicago, 1975); bibliographies, directories, and technical publications. It has issued a very helpful series of basic manuals on techniques for archives and manuscripts, including Maynard Brichford, *Appraisal and Accessioning* (Chicago, 1977); David B. Gracy II, *Arrangement and Description* (1977); Sue E. Holbert, *Reference and Access* (1977); Timothy Walch, *Security* (1977); John Fleckner, *Surveys* (1977); Gail Farr Casterline, *Exhibits* (1980); H. Thomas Hickerson, *An Introduction to Automated Access* (1981); Ralph E. Ehrenberg, *Maps and Architectural Drawings* (1982); Ann E. Pederson and Gail Farr Casterline, *Public Programs* (1982); Carolyn Hoover Sung, *Reprography* (1982); Mary Lynn Ritzenthaler, *Conservation* (1983); Ritzenthaler, Gerald Munoff, and Margery S. Long, *Administration of Photographic Collections* (1984); and Margaret L. Hedstrom, *Machine-Readable Records* (1984). The Society has also issued a publication on *Evaluation of Archival Institutions: Services, Principles, and Guide to Self-Study* (1982).

The *Association for Information and Image Management* (AIIM), formerly the National Micrographics Association, has issued a series of technical publications in the area of micrographics, as discussed in Chapter VII above. It also issues, and periodically updates, helpful, informative manuals on various aspects of micrographics and automation. These include: *An Introduction to Micrographics; Glossary of Micrographics; An Introduction to Microform Indexing and Retrieval Systems; Microfilm in Records Management; and A Microfilm Handbook,* an illustrated directory of microfilm equipment.

Other publications

H.G. Jones, *Local Government Records: An Introduction to Their Management, Preservation, and Use* (Nashville: American Association for State and Local History, 1980) is the only book that focuses exclusively on local government records management and archival programs. Two standard works on records management are William Benedon, *Records Management* (Englewood Cliffs: Prentice Hall, 1969) and Emmet J. Leahy and Christopher A. Cameron, *Modern Records Management* (New York: McGraw-Hill, 1976). More up to date, and including information on modern technological advances, are two excellent books, Wilmer O. Maedke, Mary F. Robek, and Gerald F. Brown, *Information and Records Management* (Encino, CA: Glencoe, 1981) and Violet S. Thomas, Dexter R. Schubert, and JoAnn Lee, *Records Management: Systems and Administration* (New York: Wiley and Sons, 1983).

In addition to the AIIM publications noted above, William L. Saffady, *Micrographics* (Littleton, Colorado: Libraries Unlimited, 1978) is a good introduction to that topic. The National Center for State Courts' *Microfilm and the Courts:*

Guide for Court Managers (Williamsburg: National Center for State Courts, 1976) provides practical advice on establishing a microfilm program. The International City Management Association's *Records Management and Information Retrieval: Developing a Micrographics System for Local Government* (Washington: The International City Management Association, *Management Information Service Report* Vol. VII, no. 5, May, 1975) provides a good introduction and overview.

George Cunha, *Conservation of Library Materials* (2 vols., Metuchen, NJ: Scarecrow Press, 1972) is a good overview of that topic. Judith Fortson-Jones, *A Manual for Records Preservation and Disaster Planning for Local Government Agencies in Nebraska* (Lincoln: Nebraska State Historical Society, 1981) is an easy to read practical manual. Peter Waters' manual, *Procedures of Salvage of Water-Damaged Library Materials* (Washington: Library of Congress, 1979) provides helpful information on how to deal with water-soaked records.

James R. Griesemer, *Microcomputers In Local Government* (Washington: International City Management Association, 1983) is a good introduction to this rapidly-changing area. Donald F. Norris, *Microcomputers and Local Government: A Handbook* (Looseleaf, Omaha, University of Nebraska, 1984) is a clearly written, practical handbook that explains how to plan for adoption of microcomputer technology. William Saffady, *The Automated Office: An Introduction to the Technology* (Silver Spring, MD: National Micrographics Association, 1981) is a good general introduction to automation. The National Center for State Courts' manual *Automated Information Systems: Implementation Guidelines* (n.p., National Center for State Courts, 1983) is a clearly written account of how to carry out a systems analysis and develop an automated system. Stephen B. Geller, *Care and Handling of Computer Magnetic Storage Media* (Washington: National Bureau of Standards, Government Printing Office, 1983) provides information on preservation of machine-readable records.

Periodicals

In addition to the journals and newsletters of professional organizations, a few magazines and periodicals carry articles, news, and advertising of interest to records and information managers, including those in local governments. Some of these are available free upon request; for others, there is a subscription charge. These periodicals include:

The Office, Office Publications, Inc., 1600 Summer Street, Stamford, CN 06904. Advertising of new products and services and articles on office management, equipment, and automation.

Information Management, PTN Publishing Corporation, 101 Crossways Park West, Woodbury, NY 11797. News and articles on information systems, technology, software and media.

Microfilm Techniques, 250 Fulton Ave., Hempstead, NY 11550. News on new products and articles on microfilm applications.

Consultants

Some local goverments have found outside expert consultation advantageous, especially when planning a program or when dealing with technical areas like computer technology. An experienced consultant can bring knowledge of records administration techniques, insights gained from association with other programs that have proven successful, understanding of legal requirements, and up-to-date knowledge of technological advances. A consultant may also bring the outsider's objectivity and persuasive analysis that may be needed to convince government decision makers that a records administration or archival program is needed. On the other hand, consultation is usually expensive, and the intervention of a consultant usually provides only a report and a plan for action, not the action itself. It is up to the government to implement the consultant's advice and recommendations.

In seeking and selecting a consultant, local governments should give preference to an individual or firm with considerable experience with government records or institutional records programs. It is advisable to ask for references, and to check them, to ensure reliability and expertise. It is essential to have a contract with the consultant that specifies exactly what is expected and a deadline for completing the required report or other work.

Appendix I

State Offices with Responsibility for, or Information on, Local Government Records

The state agencies listed below have the legal responsibility for retention and disposition of local government records in their states, or provide advice and assistance on records management, or can furnish information on where to turn for assistance.

Alabama
Department of Archives and History
624 Washington Avenue
Montgomery, AL 36130
(205) 261-4361

Alaska
State Archives
P.O. Box C-0207
Juneau, AK 99811
(907) 465-2275

Arizona
Department of Library, Archives & Public Records
1700 West Washington
State Capitol
Phoenix, AZ 85007
(602) 255-4035

Arkansas
Arkansas History Commission
One Capitol Mall
Little Rock, AK 72201
(501)371-2141

California
State Archives
Office of the Secretary of State
1020 "O" Street
Sacramento, CA 95814
(916) 445-4293

Colorado
Division of State Archives and Public Records
1313 Sherman Street, 1-B20
Denver, CO 80203
(303) 866-2055

Connecticut
Archives, History & Genealogy Section
State Library
231 Capitol Avenue
Hartford, CT 06106
(203) 566-3690 or 3692

Delaware
Bureau of Archives and Records Management
Hall of Records
Dover, DE 19901
(302) 736-5318

Florida
Bureau of Archives and Records Management
Division of Library & Information Services
Department of State
R.A. Gray Building
500 South Bronough Street
Tallahassee, FL 32301-8020
(904) 487-2073

Georgia
Georgia Department of Archives & History
330 Capitol Avenue, South East
Atlanta, GA 30334
(404) 656-2358

Hawaii
State Archives
Iolani Palace Grounds
Honolulu, HI 96813
(808) 548-2355

Idaho
Idaho State Historical Society
610 North Julia Davis Drive
Boise, ID 83702
(208) 334-3890

Illinois
State Archives
Office of the Secretary of State
Archives Building
Springfield, IL 62756
(217) 782-4682

Indiana
Indiana Commission on Public Records
Room 501, State Office Building
Indianapolis, IN 46204
(317) 232-3373

Iowa
State Historical Society
Iowa State Historical Department
East 7th & Court Avenue
Des Moines, IA 50319
(515) 281-3007

Kansas
Kansas State Historical Society
120 West Tenth
Topeka, KS 66612
(913) 296-3251

Kentucky
Kentucky Department for Libraries & Archives
Public Records Division
Box 537
Frankfort, KY 40602
(502) 875-7000

Louisiana
Archives and Records Service
Department of State
P.O. Box 94125
Baton Rouge, LA 70804-9125
(504) 342-5440

Maine
State Archives
Capitol-Station House 84
Augusta, ME 04333
(207) 289-5790

Maryland
State Archives
350 Rowe Boulevard
Annapolis, MD 21401
(301) 269-3915

Massachusetts
State Archives and Records Division
Office of the Secretary of State
220 Morrissey Boulevard
Boston, MA 02125
(617) 727-2816

Michigan
Department of State
History Bureau, State Archives
3405 North Logan
Lansing, MI 48918
(517) 335-9168

Minnesota
Minnesota Historical Society
1500 Mississippi Street
St. Paul, MN 55101
(612) 296-6980

Mississippi
Department of Archives and History
P.O. Box 571
Jackson, MS 39205
(601) 359-1424

Missouri
Records Management and Archives Service
1001 Industrial Drive
Jefferson City, MO 65101
(314) 751-4502

Montana
Archives and Library Division
Montana Historical Society
225 North Roberts Street
Helena, MT 59620
(406) 444-2694

Nebraska
Nebraska State Historical Society
Box 82554
Lincoln, NE 68501
(402) 471-4783

Records Management Division
P.O. Box 94921
Lincoln, NE 68509
(402) 471-2559

Nevada
Division of Archives and Records
101 South Fall Street
Carson City, NV 89710
(702) 885-5210

New Hampshire
Division of Records Management and Archives
71 South Fruit Street
Concord, NH 03301
(603) 271-2236

New Jersey
Division of Archives & Records Management
CN 307, 2300 Stuyvesant Avenue
Trenton, NJ 08625
(609) 530-3200

New Mexico
State Records Center and Archives
404 Montezuma
Santa Fe, NM 87503
(505) 827-8860

New York
State Archives and Records Administration
State Education Department
10A46 Cultural Education Center
Albany, NY 12230
(518) 474-1195

North Carolina
Department of Cultural Resources
Division of Archives and History
109 East Jones Street
Raleigh, NC 27611
(919) 733-7305

North Dakota
State Historical Society of North Dakota
North Dakota Heritage Center
Bismarck, ND 58505-0179
(701) 224-2668

Records Management Division
Office of Management and Budget
State Capitol
Bismarck, ND 58505
(701) 224-3579

Ohio
Ohio Historical Society
1985 Velma Avenue
Columbus, OH 43211
(614) 297-2350

Oklahoma
Oklahoma Resources Branch
Oklahoma Department of Libraries
200 North East 18th Street
Oklahoma City, OK 73105
(405) 521-2502

Oregon
Archives Division
Secretary of State
1005 Broadway, N.E.
Salem, OR 97310
(503) 378-4242

Pennsylvania
Pennsylvania Historical and Museum Commission
P.O. Box 1026
Harrisburg, PA 17108-1026
(717) 787-2891

Rhode Island
Department of Administration
State Records Center
83 Park Street
Providence, RI 02903
(401) 277-2283

South Carolina
South Carolina Department of Archives & History
1430 Senate Street
P.O. Box 11669
Columbia, SC 29211
(803) 734-8577

South Dakota
State Records Management Program
State Capitol Building
Pierre, SD 57501-5075
(605) 773-3589

Tennessee
Tennessee State Library & Archives
403 7th Avenue North
Nashville, TN 37219
(615) 741-2764

Texas
Texas State Library
P.O. Box 12927, Capitol Station
Austin, TX 78711
(512) 463-5480

Utah
Utah State Archives and Records Service
Archives Building
State Capitol
Salt Lake City, UT 84114
(801) 533-5250

Vermont
Public Records Division
State Administration Building
6 Baldwin Street
Montpelier, VT 05602
(802) 828-3288

Virginia
State Archives
Virginia State Library
11th Street Capitol Square
Richmond, VA 23219-3491
(804) 786-2332

Washington
Office of the Secretary of State
Division of Archives and Records Management
P.O. Box 9000
Olympia, WA 98504-9000
(206) 753-5485

West Virginia
Department of Culture and History
Cultural Center-Capitol Complex
Charleston, WV 25305
(304) 348-0230

Wisconsin
State Historical Society
816 State Street
Madison, WI 53716
(608) 262-7304

Wyoming
State Archives
Museums & Historical Department
Barrett Building
Cheyenne, WY 82002
(307) 777-7013

Index

Access: and retrieval, 72
Active records: stage in life-cycle, 38; purposes of, 53; controlling, 53-63; organizing, 53-63
American National Standards Institute (ANSI), 85, 88-89
Aperture cards, 88
Appraisal: process of, 44-45, 47; primary values of, 45-46; secondary values of, 46-47; of machine-readable records, 100, 102-3; of archival records, 104, 112
Archival program, 111-12, 116
Archival records: defined, 9, 39; and records officer, 15; and advisory board, 16; and history, 19, 108-9; preserving, 19, 112-13; and state offices, 21, 22; categories of, 47-49; and active records program, 68, 78; misconceptions about, 104-5; benefits of, 105-6; as legal documents, 106-7; as research tools, 108-9; responsibilty for, 110-11; storage of, 112-13; arranging, 113-15; describing, 113-15; promoting, 115-16
Archives. See Archival records
Archivists: and computers, 95
Associations, as resource: local government, 120-21; national, 122-25; publications of, 127-28

Brichford, M., 48

Community history: and archives, 19, 109, 117-18
Computer-assisted retrieval (CAR) systems, 87-88
Computer disks, 3, 99
Computer output microfilm (COM), 90-91
Computers: applications of, 5, 9, 93-94; and records officer, 15; and inactive records program, 70; and microfilm, 87-88, 90-91; technology and, 92-93; problems with, 94-96; determining need for, 96-98; costs, 97-98, 101; and documentation, 98; and care of machine-readable records, 99
Computer tapes, 3, 70, 99
Consultants, 130-31
Control of active records: and correspondence, 53-54; and reports, 54, 56; and forms, 56-57; and filing systems, 56-62; and Freedom of Information, 62-63; and vital records, 63
Copies, extra. See Duplication
Correspondence: management of, 53-54
Costs: low, as a goal, 9-10, 38, 56-57; and "Guardians of the Public Record," 17; and forms, 56-57; and inactive records, 66-67; and microfilm, 82; and computers, 97-98, 101
Creation: of records, 3, 7

143

Cubic foot equivalents, 34, 36

Destruction: of records, 7, 10, 15
Diazo film, 86
Disposal: and microfilm, 83
Disposition: as part of management, 7; and legal guidelines, 9, 20; schedule for, 23, 28-29, 37; planning for, 38-39; stages of, 38-39; advantages of, 40, 51; state's role in, 40-41, 44; implementing, 50-51; reports of, 51; and filing systems, 61; of inactive records, 72. *See also* Destruction; Disposal
Documentation: and computers, 98
Dry silver film, 85-86
Duplication: and inventory results, 29, 34; convenience files, 59; avoiding, 60-62; and microfilm, 82, 90
Duplication and dispersal, 63

Equipment: storage, 65

Family history: and archival records, 19, 109
Federal government: publications of, 126-27
Filing systems: and schedules, 23; and records series, 25; arranging, 58; types of, 58, 59; factors for success in, 60-62; and archives, 113
Finding aids, 114-15
Forms: inventory, 26-27, 31-35; management of 56-57; and active records program, 68; and inactive records program, 71, 74-75; sample, 74-75
Freedom of Information: and record control and organization, 62-63; and machine-readable records, 101

Government history: and archives, 108
Government leaders: support of, 16-18
"Guardians of the Public Record," 16

Haller, S.E., 77, 79
Humidity controls: and storage, 4, 69-70; and inventory, 29; and machine-readable records, 99; and archives, 113

Inactive records: defined, 9; management of, 10. 15, 65-79; and the law, 13; storage of, 68-70; transfer of, 70-71, 73-77; disposition of, 72; retention of, 72-73
Inactive records program: advantages of, 65-67; coordination of, 67-68; and storage center, 68-70; management of, 70-72
Inventory: and records management officer, 15; results of, 23, 28-30; aims of, 25-26; conducting, 27-28; form for, 26-27, 29; report on, 30; and schedule, 37; and active records program, 68
Inventory form, 26-27

Jones, H.G., 117

Law: as basis for management program, 13-14, 18, 20, 22; and microfilm, 84; and archives, 110-11
Legal rights: and archival records, 106-7
Local government: role of in retention and disposition, 41, 43; as resource, 119-21; 125-26

Index

Machine-readable records: and state guidelines, 95; care of, 99; scheduling, 99-101
Magnetic tape, 101
Maintenance: of records, 3, 7
Microcomputers, 92, 96. *See also* Computers
Microfiche, 87-88, 90
Microfilm: use of, 3, 5, 9; and law, 20; and inventory, 29, 39; and records management program, 40, 78; and vital records, 63; temperature and humidity and, 70; as information mangement tool, 80-82; benefits of, 80, 82; limitations of, 82-83; planning for, 83-85; types of, 85-86; and computers, 87-88, 90-91; quality of, 88-91
Micrographics, 15, 80-91. *See also* Microfilm
Montgomery County, Ohio, 77-79

New York State Archives: inventory form of, 31-35

Ordinance: for records management, 13, 23. *See also* Law
Organization: need for, of active records, 3,7; and correspondence, 53-54; and reports, 54, 56; and forms, 56-57; and filing systems, 56-62; and Freedom of Information, 62-63; and vital records, 63

Privacy: and Freedom of Information, 62-63; and machine-readable records, 101
Publications: as resources, 16, 125-31

Records: retrieving, 3; defined, 3-4; creating, 3, 7; maintaining, 3, 7; organizing, 3, 7; as resources, 5-7; values of, 6-7, 19; types of, 9; disposition of, 7, 15, 20, 38-51; obsolete, 28; destruction of, 39; retention of, 38-51; appraising, 44-47; archival, 39, 47-49, 104-18; and micrographics, 80-91; and computers, 92-103; machine-readable, 99-101; resources for help with, 119-31. *See also* Active records; Archival records; Inactive records
Records access officer, 62-63
Records advisory board, 16
Records Center Transfer List, 71, 76-77
Records keeping: problems of, 4-5
Records management office: and inventory, 27-30; and disposition, 41
Records management officer: responsibilities of, 14-16; and inventory, 23, 27; and disposition, 51; and inactive records program, 68, 70-72; and computers, 95
Records management program: objects of, 7; elements of, 8-9; benefits of, 10; foundations of, 13-16
Records series: transfering, 73
Records storage center: purpose of, 65; planning for, 68-70
Records Transfer List (City of Rochester), 73-77
Reports: inventory, 30; of records disposition, 51; control of, 54, 56
Research: historical, 6, 10, 41, 108-9; and archives, 108-9, 115
Resources: local governments, 119; for records problems, 119-31; state governments as, 120;

associations of local government officials, 120-21; national associations, 122-25; publications, 125-31

Retention: schedules for, 23, 28, 37; advantages of, 40; state's role in, 40-41, 44; sample schedule of, 42-43; implementing, 50-51; and filing systems, 61; of inactive records, 72; and microfilm, 84; of machine-readable records, 100

Retrieval: faster, 67; access and, 72

Schedules: disposition, 23, 28, 35, 37; retention, 23, 28, 35, 37, 42-43; and inventory, 37; state published, 41; sample retention, 42-43; and machine-readable records, 99-101

Security: of storage center, 69; and microfilm, 82; of archives, 112

Series, records, 25-27

Service bureau: and microfilm, 84; and computers, 97-98

Shelving, 7, 112

Silver halide film, 85-86

Social history: and archives, 109

Space (storage), 10

State government: and archives, 19, 21; role of in management, 19-22; role of in retention and disposition, 41, 43; as resource, 120

State guidelines: and computers, 95-96

State law: and archives, 110-11. *See also* Law

Storage: problems of, 4-5; space for, 10; equipment for, 29; secure, 65; and microfilm, 90; of archives, 112

Support: public, 19

Survey: informal, 25-26

Technology. *See* Computers; Microfilm

Temperature controls: and inventory, 29; in storage centerr, 69-71; and machine-readable records, 99; and archives, 113

Transfer: instructions for, 73, 76-77; form for, 74-75

Transparent electrophotographic (TEP) film, 85-86

Vesicular film, 86

Vital records, 9, 63